U0800500

高等院校电子商务专业规划教材

跨境电子商务基础与实务

（中英双语版）

徐　凡　主　编

朱　臻　刘　翚　副主编

中国铁道出版社有限公司
CHINA RAILWAY PUBLISHING HOUSE CO., LTD.

内 容 简 介

本书按照理论与实践相结合、市场原理与现实案例相统一的原则，系统阐释了跨境电子商务最新实务操作与商业模式。并以杭州、重庆为例，深度分析现阶段我国跨境电商行业的问题与市场挑战，同时总结跨境电子商务相关法律法规与风险控制核心经典方法。本书内容全面、体系完备，理论与实操相得益彰，旨在使读者全面理解、掌握跨境电子商务的基本理论、实践规范和趋势规律等，力求突出新理论、新知识、新技术和新方法，以培养、提升学习者开拓创新能力。另外，每章文后均配备时效性思考题，强化学习者综合商务素养与批判性思维能力。

本书适合作为国际贸易、国际经济、国际工商管理、商务英语等专业本科三年级及硕士一年级的教材，也可作为广大商务人士跨境电子商务培训教材，以及行业从业者自修提高的参考用书。

图书在版编目（CIP）数据

跨境电子商务基础与实务：中英双语版/徐凡主编. —北京：中国铁道出版社，2019.1（2021.12重印）

高等院校电子商务专业规划教材

ISBN 978-7-113-25458-2

Ⅰ.①跨… Ⅱ.①徐… Ⅲ.①电子商务-高等学校-教材-汉、英 Ⅳ.①F713.36

中国版本图书馆CIP数据核字（2019）第018883号

书　　名：跨境电子商务基础与实务（中英双语版）
作　　者：徐　凡

策划编辑：周海燕　　编辑部电话：（010）51873090
责任编辑：周海燕　李学敏
封面设计：乔　楚
责任校对：张玉华
责任印制：樊启鹏

出版发行：中国铁道出版社有限公司（100054，北京市西城区右安门西街8号）
网　　址：http://www.tdpress.com/51des/
印　　刷：北京柏力行彩印有限公司
版　　次：2019年1月第1版　2021年12月第3次印刷
开　　本：787 mm × 1 092 mm　1/16　印张：10.5　字数：198千
书　　号：ISBN 978-7-113-25458-2
定　　价：39.00元

版权所有　侵权必究

凡购买铁道版图书，如有印制质量问题，请与本社教材图书营销部联系调换。电话：（010）63550836

打击盗版举报电话：市电（010）63549461

前　言

跨境电子商务（又称“跨境电商”）是电子商务的一种特殊形式，通常指分属不同关境的交易主体，通过电子商务平台达成交易，进行支付结算，并通过跨境物流送达商品、完成交易的一种国际商业活动。跨境电子商务是电子商务应用的更高级形式，其充分利用现代信息技术，正在与实体经济加速融合，对人们的日常生产、生活和消费产生深刻影响。因为不同国家或地区的贸易双方均可通过互联网或者相关信息平台实现这一交易，所以跨境电商已日益成为信息化、网络化、市场化、国际化条件下配置资源的重要途径，以及引领经济社会发展进步的一种重要力量。

近年来，随着电子商务迅猛普及，很多高校相继开设电子商务相关课程，跨境电商课程也成为高等院校国际贸易、财经等专业选修课。就其本质而言，跨境电子商务课程内容贴近进出口实务，且与电子商务相结合，是一门标准复合型商务课程。鉴于大量涌现的行业术语及理论，教材以中英文双语进行编写势在必行，然囿于师资力量相对短缺，本课程鲜有双语版教材在国内出版面世。鉴于行业与学科的明确发展趋势，以及市场对于跨境电商人才的迫切需求，我们设计推出本书，以便于教学与研究。

本书重点阐述跨境电子商务基本原理和实务操作流程与规范。第一、二章分别概述电子商务和跨境电子商务的定义、代表性特征、分类及分类标准、发展现状等；第三章以图表形式介绍操作模式，包括操作模式的特点和流程；第四章着重探讨跨境电子商务五种不同商业模式（包括 B2C，B2B，C2C，C2B 和 BMC）；第五章结合实例介绍与分析跨境电商多种交易、支付平台以及如何自建平台；第六章围绕国际物流服务平台主题，除介绍不同平台、分类及分类标准外，还着重补充主要国际快运公司信息及选择跨境物流模式；第七章结合最新电子数据交换（EDI）、大数据（Big Data）、云计算（Cloud Computing）和信息与通信技术（ICT），阐述跨境电商与新技术的相关影响与依赖；第八、九章分别以杭州和重庆为例，分析跨境电子商务的最新发展、现状与现实问题；第十章分析海关手续、相应法律规章问题、在线纠纷解决体系等跨境电子商务风险与挑战；第十一章展望未来，分析跨境电商的演绎趋势与前景。

本书内容全面、体系完备，理论与实操相得益彰，旨在使读者全面理解、掌握跨境电子商务的基本理论、实践规范和趋势规律等，力求突出新理论、新知识、新技术和新方法，以培养和提升学习者开拓创新能力。每章核心英文术语均配有详细中文释义，以要点概述形式进行概念定义、解读或延伸阐述，便于高效掌握知识要点及举一反三。另外，每章文后均配备时效性思考题，以提高学习者综合商务素养与批判性思维能力。

本书适合作为高等院校国际贸易、国际经济、国际工商管理、商务英语等专业本科三年级及硕士一年级教材，也可用作广大商务人士跨境电子商务培训教材，以及行业从业者自修提高的参考用书。使用者既可按照目录顺序安排一个学期教学进度（需 60 ～ 80 课时），也可根据需要选择个别章节进行针对性专题学习与讨论。

本书在编写过程中参阅了国内外相关专著和教材，相关参考内容已列入文后参考文献，在此向诸位作者表示衷心谢意。此外，由于编者水平有限、时间不足，作为跨境电子商务领域双语探索性教材，本书不足之处在所难免，希望业内专家、读者不吝赐教指正。

编　者

2018 年 9 月

目　录

◎ **Chapter 1　Overview of E-commerce** ········· 1

1.1　Concept ········· 2

1.2　Characteristics ········· 4

1.2.1　Market globalization ········· 4

1.2.2　The speed of transaction ········· 5

1.2.3　The virtualization of transactions ········· 6

1.2.4　Low cost ········· 6

1.2.5　Transaction continuity ········· 7

1.3　Classification ········· 8

1.3.1　Classification by the participants in the transaction ········· 8

1.3.2　Classification by technology adopted ········· 10

1.3.3　Classification by related goods ········· 11

1.4　Development history ········· 12

1.4.1　Overall situation ········· 12

1.4.2　Development process of global e-commerce ········· 14

◎ **Chapter 2　Overview of Cross-border E-commerce** ········· 21

2.1　The definition of cross-border e-commerce ········· 21

2.2　The characteristic of cross-border e-commerce ········· 23

2.3　The classification of cross-border e-commerce ········· 27

2.4　The development present situation in China ········· 28

2.4.1　Market size ········· 28

2.4.2　Scale structure ········· 29

2.4.3　Target market ········· 30

◎ **Chapter 3 Operating Mode** …… 33

3.1 Graphic of operating mode …… 33

3.2 The characteristics of operating mode …… 34

3.2.1 Deepen of the electric business industry …… 34

3.2.2 Integrated marketing …… 34

3.2.3 Basis of large data …… 35

3.3 The operating mode of foreign trade imports and foreign trade exports …… 36

3.3.1 Foreign trade imports …… 36

3.3.2 Foreign trade exports …… 37

3.4 The process of operation …… 38

3.4.1 Logistics …… 38

3.4.2 Capital flows …… 39

3.4.3 The flow of management …… 41

3.4.4 Information flow …… 43

◎ **Chapter 4 Business Model of Cross-border E-commerce** …… 45

4.1 Development status …… 45

4.2 Business model …… 45

4.2.1 Business to customer …… 46

4.2.2 Business to business …… 48

4.2.3 Customer to customer …… 49

4.2.4 Consumer to business …… 50

4.2.5 Business-Medium-Consumer …… 52

4.3 Comparison of the main modes of cross-border e-commerce …… 52

◎ **Chapter 5 Platform of Cross-border E-commerce** …… 55

5.1 Concept of cross-border e-commerce …… 55

5.2 Trading platform …… 57

5.2.1 eBay …… 57

5.2.2 Haitao.com …… 58

5.2.3 Amazon …… 59

5.3 Payment platform ··· 60

5.3.1 Electronic payment ··· 60

5.3.2 PayPal ··· 61

5.3.3 Alipay ··· 62

5.4 Self-built cross-border e-commerce platform model ··· 63

5.4.1 Concept ··· 63

5.4.2 Advantages ··· 64

◎ **Chapter 6 International Logistics Services Pattern** ··· 67

6.1 Concept of cross-border logistics ··· 67

6.2 Classification of cross-border Logistics ··· 67

6.2.1 Third-party logistics ··· 68

6.2.2 Fourth party logistics ··· 71

6.2.3 Overseas warehousing ··· 71

6.3 Main international express ··· 73

6.3.1 DHL express ··· 73

6.3.2 United Parcel Service ··· 74

6.3.3 Express mail service ··· 75

6.4 The selection of cross-border logistics mode ··· 75

6.4.1 Cross-border e-commerce export logistics mode ··· 76

6.4.2 Cross-border e-commerce import logistics mode ··· 77

◎ **Chapter 7 Technology of Cross-border E-commerce** ··· 79

7.1 Electronic data interchange ··· 79

7.1.1 Definition ··· 79

7.1.2 Characteristic ··· 80

7.1.3 Challenges in EDI implementation ··· 81

7.2 Big Data ··· 82

7.2.1 Definition ··· 82

7.2.2 Characteristics ··· 83

7.2.3 Cross-border e-commerce credit evaluation system based on Big Data ··· 84

7.3 Cloud computing ······ 87
7.3.1 Definition ······ 87
7.3.2 Cloud computing and environment ······ 88
7.4 Information and communication technology ······ 90
7.4.1 Definition ······ 90
7.4.2 ICT development index ······ 91

◎ **Chapter 8 Cross-border E-commerce in Hangzhou** ······ 95
8.1 Development status ······ 95
8.1.1 Institutional mechanism innovation guarantee ······ 95
8.1.2 Rapid growth in business size ······ 96
8.1.3 The industrial system is gradually enriched ······ 97
8.2 Major constraints for cross-border e-commerce in Hangzhou ······ 98
8.2.1 Policy orientation is unclear ······ 98
8.2.2 Regulation and staffing cannot meet the needs ······ 99
8.2.3 Fierce competition among the pilot cities ······ 100
8.3 Suggestions on the further development ······ 101
8.3.1 Improve business scale and logistics efficiency ······ 101
8.3.2 Vigorously promote and expand the influence of pilot ······ 102
8.3.3 Explore cross-border trade export business ······ 102

◎ **Chapter 9 Cross-border E-commerce in Chongqing** ······ 105
9.1 Development status ······ 105
9.1.1 The exponential growth of cross-border e-commerce trading ······ 106
9.1.2 Cross-border logistics ······ 106
9.1.3 Customs supervision mode ······ 107
9.2 Analysis of existing problems ······ 108
9.2.1 Cross-border logistics restricts the development of cross-border e-commerce ······ 108
9.2.2 Regulatory standards still need to be improved ······ 109
9.2.3 Shortage of talents ······ 110

9.3 Related recommendations ······ 110
9.3.1 Give full play to the advantages of location ······ 110
9.3.2 Strengthen the supply chain construction of cross-border e-commerce ······ 111
9.3.3 Strengthen the supervision of cross-border e-commerce market ······ 112
9.3.4 Strengthen the introduction and cultivation of cross-border e-commerce talents ······ 113

◎ Chapter 10 Threats and Challenges ······ 115
10.1 Customs formality, legal and regulatory issues ······ 115
10.1.1 Customs formality ······ 115
10.1.2 Legal and regulatory issues ······ 116
10.2 Online Dispute Resolution ······ 117
10.2.1 Introduction ······ 117
10.2.2 Online dispute resolution procedure ······ 117
10.3 Talent cultivation ······ 119
10.3.1 Introduction ······ 119
10.3.2 Training cross-border e-commerce talents ······ 121

◎ Chapter 11 Prospect of Cross-border E-commerce ······ 123
11.1 The trend of economic development under the new situation ······ 124
11.2 More profits in the foreign trade market ······ 126
11.3 Great space for development ······ 128

Glossary ······ 131

References ······ 156

Chapter 1
Overview of E-commerce

Cross-border electronic business is a special form of e-commerce. Before the study of Cross-border electronic business, we first do an overview of e-commerce. With the rapid development and application of the new generation of information technology such as Internet of things, cloud computing and mobile terminals, e-commerce, as a new-type business model, is accelerating its integration with the substantial economy, which has a profound impact on people's daily production, life and consumption. E-commerce has become an important way for resource allocation under the condition of informatization and networking, marketization and internationalization and an important force to lead the development and progress of economy and society. Developing e-commerce vigorously has become an strategic trend of the world's countries and regions to enhance competitiveness and seize the opportunity to develop.

要点概述

跨境电商是电子商务的一种特殊形式，在研究跨境电商之前，首先对电子商务进行概述。随着物联网、云计算和移动终端等新一代信息技术的飞速发展和应用的日益普及，电子商务作为一种新型商业模式，正在与实体经济加速融合，对人们的日常生产、生活和消费产生深刻影响，并且已经成为信息化、网络化、市场化、国际化条件下配置资源的重要途径，成为引领经济社会发展进步的一种重要力量。大力发展电子商务，成为世界各国、各地区提高竞争力，抢占发展先机的战略举措。

In recent years, China's e-commerce maintains a rapid developing trend.Online consumer groups grow rapidly.The e-commerce market scale is expanding. In 2015, China's e-commerce turnover amounted to 15.8 trillion yuan by an increase of 30.4% and the network retail market transaction reached the size of 3.8 trillion yuan by an increase of 35.7%.The market size has surpassed that of the United States, becoming the world's largest network retail market. E-commerce has become an important social economic form and circulation mode in our country, which plays an increasingly important role in the development of national economy and society.[1]

要点概述

近年来，中国电子商务保持着快速发展的趋势。在线消费群体迅速增长。电子商务市场规模不断扩大。2015 年，中国电子商务交易额达到 15.8 万亿元，增长 30.4%；网络零售市场交易额达到 3.8 万亿元，增长 35.7%。市场规模已超过美国，成为全球最大的网络零售市场。电子商务已成为中国重要的社会经济形态和流通方式，对国民经济和社会的发展起着越来越重要的作用。

Marco Gervasi, the founder of Niki business consulting company, believes that China has a relatively perfect IT technology architecture. If the power of IoT integration index data is added to the complex network, the innovative development of e-commerce and IoT will be promoted at the same time. China will not just lead the world in e-commerce, but could also become a leader in the IoT model.

要点概述

奈基商务咨询公司创始人 Marco Gervasi 认为：中国有比较完善的 IT 技术架构，若是在复杂的网络中加入物联网整合指数级数据的力量，将同时推动电商和物联网的创新发展。电商不会是中国领先世界的唯一领域，中国还有可能成为物联网模式的领导者。

1.1 Concept

Electronic commerce is a new type of transaction that appeared in the early years of the century. Since the beginning of the 21st century, electronic commerce has been widely used in various fields with a high developing speed, which has greatly impacted the traditional trade mode. Due to the wide coverage of electronic commerce and constantly new problems and solutions, so far, the electronic commerce does not have an exact definition. Scholars from various industries and countries have given different definitions from their own professional perspectives. "E-commerce is a very broad concept, but also a very simple and straightforward one" , said Wang Haipeng, CEO of Pontian

[1] 聂林海．我国电子商务发展的特点和趋势［J］．中国流通经济，2014，28(06)：97-101.

Information System (Beijing) Company. It is the process of automation and optimization of various business models by information technology. Therefore, it is not only about online transactions, but actually covers almost all business behaviors of enterprises and individuals. Cui Jian, executive vice general manager of Beijing Fangzheng Education E-commerce Company, said in a speech entitled "Healthy E-commerce Mode" that all commodity transaction activities and services conducted in the form of electronic information network can be attributed to e-commerce.

要点概述

到目前为止，电子商务都没有一个公认的确切的定义，各个行业和各国学者站在自己的专业角度给出了很多不一样的定义。蓬天信息系统(北京)有限公司的CEO王海蓬说，真正的电子商务是一个非常广泛的概念，也是很简单很直接的概念。就是信息技术对各种商业模式的自动化与优化的过程，所以它绝不仅仅是在网上做交易，它实际上涵盖了企业、个人几乎所有的商业行为。北京方正人教电子商务有限公司执行副总经理崔建在题为“健康的电子商务模式”演讲中则说，凡是以电子形式在信息网络上进行的商品交易活动和服务都可以归结为电子商务。

Although CEOs have different explanation to the electronic commerce, the idea that business is prior to electronics is consistent. Zhang Ruimin, President of Haier, has mentioned that the key to e-commerce is business.The President of the Beijing iBASE software corporation has made it clear that the core of e-commerce is still business, but the means is electronic, which is to make the entire business trade electronic. The business process of the enterprise is being reinvented online so that the enterprise can do all the business on the Internet.

要点概述

尽管CEO们对电子商务的解释不尽相同，但先商务后电子的概念却是一致的。海尔总裁张瑞敏就提到过电子商务的关键是商务。北京国信贝斯软件有限公司总裁吴广印也明确表示电子商务核心还是商务，只不过手段是电子，也就是使整个商务贸易活动电子化，即将企业各项传统业务流程进行改造上网，使企业能在网上进行一切业务流程。

According to the definition of Baidu encyclopedia, e-commerce usually refers to a new business operation mode of online shopping, online transaction and online payment between merchants, as well as various business activities, transaction activities, financial activities and related comprehensive service activities, which is based on browser server application mode in a wide range of commercial trade activities around the world.

要点概述

根据百度百科的定义，电子商务通常是指在全球各地广泛的商业贸易活动中，在因特网开放的网络环境下，基于浏览器服务器应用方式，买卖双方不谋面地进行各种商贸活动，实现消费者的网上购物、商户之间的网上交易和在线电子支付以及各种商务活动、交易活动、金融活动和相关的综合服务活动的一种新型的商业运营模式。

1.2 Characteristics

1.2.1 Market globalization

Traditional business is a shop-style sale characterized by fixed sales locations (i.e.stores) and fixed sales time. Sales on the Internet are carried out through an online store characterized by an information bank, so its sales space extends with the extension of the network system. Without any geographical barriers, its retail time is determined by the consumer, the online user. Therefore, the sale of the internet has a new time and space advantage over the traditional sales model. This advantage can meet the needs of online users to a greater extent. In fact, the online shopping has no national boundaries. Anyone who can access the Internet, whether in South Africa or in North America, will be tolerated in one market and become a potential customer for the internet business.

要点概述

传统商业是一种以固定的销售地点（即商店）和固定的销售时间为特征的商店式销售。网络销售是通过一个以信息库为特征的网上商店进行的，其销售空间随着网络系统的扩展而扩大，没有任何地理障碍。它的零售时间是由消费者，即在线用户决定的。因此，与传统的销售模式相比，互联网的销售具有时间和空间优势。这一优势可以在更大程度上满足在线用户的需求。事实上，网上购物没有国界。任何可以上网的人，无论是在南非还是在北美，都可以融入一个市场，并成为互联网业务的潜在客户。

An obvious example is the sale of books. Traditional book sales are established in a certain area. A bookstore stores a certain amount of books. Consumers only go to the bookstore to search for and purchase the books they need. For the merchant, his customer base is limited to the consumers in the region. The emergence of e-commerce enables consumers to stay at home, stroll around the global online bookstore, browse, read and search for books and materials that they love and need, obtaining information to the maximum extent. For merchants, e-commerce can be an approach to sell their products to consumers around the world. Therefore, the potential customer base has undoubtedly reached its maximum. In less than four years from the end of 1994 when it was founded to 1997 when its stock went public, Amazon, a US on-line book company, sold books in 160 countries and regions around the world with an increasing annual sales from zero to 148 million, which became the miracle of sales and e-commerce.

要点概述

一个明显的例子是图书的销售，传统的图书销售都是在某一个地域建立一个书店，存储一定量的图书，消费者只能到这家书店里才能搜寻和购买自己所需的图书，而对于商家来讲，他的顾客群体也只是局限于该地域的消费者。电子商务的出现可以使消费者足不出户，漫步全球的网上书店，浏览、阅读和搜寻自己所喜爱和需要的图书和资料，无疑使自己获得了最大的信息资讯；对于商家，通过电子商务可以向全世界的消费者推销自己的商品，其潜在的顾客群无疑也达到了最大。美国的网上图书公司 Amazon.com 从 1994 年底创立，到 1997 年股票正式上市的不足 4 年里，销售图书遍及世界上 160 个国家和地区，年销售额从零增至 1.48 亿美元，创造了图书销售和电子商务的奇迹。

1.2.2 The speed of transaction

Electronic commerce can instantly complete transmission and computer automatic processing in all parts of the world, without the intervention of personnel, e-commerce can be transmitted and processed automatically in the world with high transaction speed.

要点概述

电子商务能在世界各地瞬间完成传递与计算机自动处理，而且无须人员干预，交易速度快捷。

The emergence of Alipay and WeChat payment has made the payment method of electronic trade more unified, and can be used in many different situations, which further promotes the rapidization of trade.

要点概述

支付宝和微信支付的出现使得电子贸易的支付方式变得更加统一，能够在许多不同的情况下使用，这也进一步促进了贸易的快捷化。

1.2.3 The virtualization of transactions

Through the trade of the computer interconnection network represented by the Internet, the two parties can negotiate, sign, order and pay through the computer interconnection network without having to do it in person. The entire transaction is completely virtualized. Virtualization is the development trend of today's world economy. The foundation of virtualized transactions is the promotion and application of rapidly developing high-tech.

要点概述

通过以互联网为代表的计算机互联网络进行的贸易，双方从开始洽谈、签约到订货、支付等，无须当面进行，均通过计算机互联网络完成，整个交易完全虚拟化。虚拟化是当今世界经济的发展趋势，虚拟化的交易能够达成，其基础在于飞速发展的高新科技的推广运用。

Although convenient and fast, virtualized transactions bring risks to both buyers and sellers, because the virtualization of transactions aggravate the opacity of transactions, making it impossible for both parties to distinguish the authenticity of many information, thus leading to wrong judgments.

要点概述

虚拟化的交易在方便快捷的同时也给买卖双方带来了风险，因为交易的虚拟化加剧了交易的不透明性，使双方无法辨别许多信息的真实性，从而导致了错误的判断。

1.2.4 Low cost

To do business activities through the network can result a low cost of information, thus can save traffic and intermediary costs, so the whole activity cost greatly reduced. The electronic commerce redefined the traditional circulation pattern, reduced the intermediate link, made the direct transaction of the producer and the consumer possible, thus changed the whole social economy operation way to some extent.

要点概述

通过网络进行商务活动可以降低信息成本，从而节约流量和中介成本，大大降低整个活动成本。电子商务重新定义了传统的流通模式，减少了中间环节，使生产者与消费者的直接交易成为可能，从而在一定程度上改变了整个社会经济的运作方式。

For enterprises, there is no need to set up sales sites in fixed areas and hire a large number of personnel, which undoubtedly greatly reduces the expenses related to housing rental, salary expenditure, office supplies and other expenses. The sales channel has changed from the traditional wholesale model to online direct sales, which has reduced the intermediate links. Lower costs for purchasing and selling also give the goods a price advantage. For customers, the application of e-commerce saves a lot of time and cost for transportation, making it more convenient and fast to collect and sort out information, thus greatly improving the enthusiasm and possibility of purchase.

要点概述

对于企业来说，无须建立固定地域的销售场所和雇用大量的人员，大大减少了房屋租赁、工资支出、办公用品等各种相关费用的开支；销售渠道由传统模式下的层层批发到现在可以在网上直销，减少了中间环节，也降低了采购和销售的成本，使商品更具价格优势；而对于客户来说，由于电子商务的运用，省去了大量用于交通往返的时间和费用，信息的搜集和整理归纳也更加方便和快捷，因而也大大提高了购买的积极性和可能性。

1.2.5 Transaction continuity

Internet Web page, can achieve 24-hour service. Anyone can search the Web for information at any time, looking for answers to questions. The corporate web site is a permanent address that provides uninterrupted sources of information for global users.

要点概述

互联网网页可实现 24 小时服务。任何人都可以随时在网上搜索信息，寻找问题的答案。公司网站是一个为全球用户提供不间断的信息来源的永久地址。

W.W.Grainger is a major distributor of MRO products in the northern United States. In 1995, the company began to set up a trading web page on the Internet to provide e-commerce services. Since the virtual store operates 24 hours a day, 7 days a week, the products that customers can't order after the physical store is closed can now be ordered at any time, and their business volume goes up straight. Since the virtual store operates 24 hours a day, 7 days a week, customers can order goods that cannot be ordered after the physical store closes at any time now. The business volume of the store is soaring. At least 50% orders are made between 5pm and 7am the next day when the physical store closes. At least 30% of the company's online sales were repurchased by new or existing customers.

要点概述

W.W.Grainger 公司是美国北部 MRO 产品的一家主要经销商，该公司 1995 年开始在网上设立交易网页，提供电子商务的服务。由于虚拟商店是每周 7 天、每天 24 小时运作，客户本来在实体店铺关闭后不能订购的商品现在可以随时订购，其业务额直线上升，至少有 50% 的订单都是在下午 5 点到第二天清晨 7 点之间当实体商店关门后成交的，且该公司至少有 30% 的在线销售是新客户或是老客户的再次采购。

1.3 Classification

1.3.1 Classification by the participants in the transaction

1) E-commerce between enterprises and consumers (Business to Customer, B2C)

B2C is a business organization's e-commerce to consumers. This is the consumer use the Internet direct participation in the form of economic activities, similar to the commercial electronic retail business. With the advent of the Internet, online sales patterns are rapidly spreading. This form of E-commerce is generally based on the network retail industry, mainly carrying out online sales activities through the Internet.

要点概述

1）企业与消费者之间的电子商务（Business to Customer，B2C）

B2C 即表示商业机构对消费者的电子商务。这是消费者利用 Internet 直接参与经济活动的形式，类同于商业电子化的零售商务。随着 Internet 的出现，网上销售模式迅速普及。这种形式的电子商务一般以网络零售业为主，主要借助于 Internet 开展在线销售活动。

The B2C model involves a wide variety of products. There is a customer evaluation mechanism to constrain the seller and provide the seller with information that can be used for reference. It is the first choice for shopping. However, due to the large number of merchants and certain difficulties in management, the existence of black-hearted businesses cannot be avoided.

要点概述

B2C 模式涉及的商品种类繁多，有客户评价机制来约束卖家同时给卖家提供可以借鉴的信息，是购物的首选。但由于商家繁多，管理也存在一定的困难，避免不了黑心商家的存在。

2) E-commerce between Enterprise and Enterprise (Business to Business, B2B).

Business-to-business Business(B2B) is the enterprise on the Internet transactions, Business-to-business mode is the most e-commerce applications and most of the attention of a form, enterprises can use the Internet or other networks to find the best partner for each transaction, complete from the order to settle all the transaction behavior.

要点概述

2）企业间的电子商务（Business to Business，B2B）

B2B是企业在互联网上进行交易，它是电子商务应用最多和最注重的一种形式。企业可以利用互联网或其他网络为每笔交易寻找最佳合作伙伴，完成从订单到结算的所有交易行为。

B2B contains the following three elements: ① Buying and selling: B2B website or mobile platform provides consumers with high-quality and low-price products, attracting consumers to purchase and prompting more merchants to settle in. ② Cooperation: Establishing a cooperative relationship with the logistics company to provide the ultimate guarantee for the consumer's purchase behavior, which is one of the hard conditions of the B2B platform. ③ Service: Logistics is mainly to provide consumers with purchasing services to achieve another transaction.

要点概述

B2B含有以下三要素：①买卖：B2B网站或移动平台为消费者提供质优价廉的商品，吸引消费者购买的同时促使更多商家的入驻。②合作：与物流公司建立合作关系，为消费者的购买行为提供最终保障，这是B2B平台硬性条件之一。③服务：物流主要是为消费者提供购买服务，从而实现再一次的交易。

3) E-commerce between consumers and consumers (Consumer to Consumer, i.e. C2C).

C2C business platform provides an online trading platform for both buyers and sellers , so that the seller can voluntarily provide goods for online auction and the buyer can choose the products to bid. However, in the general category of e-commerce, C2C is generally an initial strategy but hardly the mainstream, and eventually will be transformed into a B2C model.

要点概述

3）消费者与消费者之间的电子商务（Consumer to Consumer，C2C）

C2C 商务平台为买卖双方提供一个在线交易平台，使卖方可以主动提供商品上网拍卖，而买方可以自行选择商品进行竞价。不过在电子商务的大范畴下，一般来说 C2C 只是一种初期的策略，难以成为主流，最终将转变成 B2C 模式。

4) C2B is the consumer to the enterprise (Customer to Business，C2B)

First popular in the United States, the core of the C2B model is to form a powerful purchasing group by aggregating a large number of users, in order to change the weak position of consumers in the one-to-one bid in the B2C model, so that a consumer can buy a single item with the price of a large wholesaler. At the same time, consumers usually customize products and prices according to their own needs, or actively participate in product design, production and pricing. Products, prices and other characteristics highlight the individual needs of consumers, and manufacturers produce customized products accordingly. At present, few domestic manufacturers really adopt this model completely.

要点概述

4) C2B 即消费者对企业（Customer to Business，C2B）

最先流行于美国，C2B 模式的核心，是通过聚合数量庞大庞大的用户形成一个强大的采购集团，以此来改变 B2C 模式中用户一对一出价的弱势地位，使之享受到以大批发商的价格买单件商品的利益。与此同时，消费者通常根据自身需求定制产品和价格，或主动参与产品设计、生产和定价，产品、价格等特征均彰显消费者的个性化需求，生产企业据此进行定制化生产。目前中国很少厂家真正完全采用这种模式。

1.3.2 Classification by technology adopted

(1) Peer-to-peer E-commerce: Peer-to-Peer (P2P), using peer-to-peer networking technology, allows users to share files and computer resources directly without having to go through a central web server. This approach does not require the involvement of the virtual market creator (Market Maker). Simply put, P2P connects people directly, allowing people to interact directly through the Internet. This makes communication on the network easier, more directly shared and interactive, and virtually eliminates intermediaries. Another important feature of P2P is to change the current Internet-centric status of the Internet, return to “decentralization” , and return power to users.

要点概述

(1) 对等电子商务：Peer-to-Peer (P2P)，使用对等网络技术，用户不需要通过中央Web服务器，可以直接共享文件和计算机资源。这种方式不需要虚拟市场创建者的介入。简单来说，P2P就是直接将人们联系起来，让人们能够通过互联网直接交互，这使得网络上的沟通变得容易、更直接共享和交互，真正地消除中间商。P2P另一个重要特点是改变互联网现在的以大网站为中心的状态、重返“非中心化”，并把权力交还给用户。

(2) Mobile e-commerce: Mobile commerce (M-commerce), which uses the mobile Internet to make online transactions by mobile devices (mobile phones, PDAs, etc.). The development potential of this model is huge and should be given full attention. Of course, this is also inseparable from the rapid development of technology and the security of users.

要点概述

(2) 移动电子商务：Mobile commerce (M-commerce)，利用移动互联网，使用移动设备（手机、掌上电脑等）进行网上交易。该模式发展潜力巨大，应给予充分重视。当然，这同时也离不开技术的快速发展以及用户安全性的保障。

1.3.3 Classification by related goods

(1) Direct e-commerce, including the provision of soft goods (also known as intangible goods) and various services to customers, such as computer software, research and advisory reports, flights, group travel and entertainment content ordering, payment, redemption and Bank-related transactions in business, securities and futures, and information services on a global scale, all of which can be transmitted directly through the network to ensure safe arrival at customers. The outstanding benefits of direct e-commerce are fast, easy and cheap, and the operating costs of enterprises are significantly reduced, which is very popular among customers. The limitation is that only goods and services suitable for transmission over the Internet can be operated.

要点概述

(1) 直接电子商务，包括向客户提供软体商品（又称无形商品）和各种服务，如计算机软件、研究性及咨询性的报告、航班、参团出游及娱乐内容的订购、支付、兑汇及银行有关业务、证券及期货的有关交易、全球规模的信息服务等，都可以通过网络直接传送，保证安全抵达客户。直接电子商务突出的好处是快速简便及十分便宜，企业的运作成本显著降低，深受客户欢迎。受限之处是只能经营适合在网上传输的商品和服务。

(2) Indirect e-commerce, including the provision of physical goods (also known as tangible commodities) and related services for clients. Because a large number of traded goods and related services in the society are required to be delivered within a wide geographical range and strict time limit, the distribution is generally completed by modern logistics distribution companies and professional service agencies. The modern logistics distribution companies and professional service organizations mentioned here are far from the warehousing and freight transport institutions and simple service departments of the traditional commerce. They are a kind of modern enterprise with a large scale and strong transportation capacity, using automated means, especially the full use of Internet information management. In this model, the use of the Internet has enabled both parties to improve their time and financial efficiency, to more efficiently obtain the goods they need and to expand the source of the merchant's customers.

要点概述

(2) 间接电子商务，包括向客户提供实体商品（又称有形商品）及有关服务。显然这是社会中大量交易的商品和有关服务。由于要求做到在很广的地域范围和严格的时限内送达，一般均交由现代物流配送公司和专业服务机构完成配送工作。这里所说的现代物流配送公司和专业服务机构远非过去传统商业的仓储货运机构和简单的服务部门，而是一种具有相当规模，拥有很强运输能力，采用自动化手段，特别是充分运用互联网信息管理的现代企业。在这种模式下，互联网的使用促使交易双方提高了时间和财务效率，能够更有效地获取到自己需要的商品，也扩大了商家的客户源。

1.4 Development history

1.4.1 Overall situation

E-commerce began in the 1960s, and rapidly grew in the 90s. Its start and rapid growth are mainly promoted by the following factors : the rapid development and wide application of computer, the gradual improvement of computer processing speed and processing capacity, the application scope is more and more extensive, for the application of e-commerce provides a foundation of network popularization and maturity, the Internet security, fast, low-cost and the growth of Internet users to promote the development of e-commerce; the popularization of electronic payment methods, electronic payment method for its convenience, fast, security and other advantages to solve the problem of payment and settlement, And thus formed a perfect global network payment and settlement system, at the same time, it also provides an important means for the network payment in e-commerce. Government's support and promotion, e-commerce receives the attention of the governments and the law, many governments have put in place supporting policies to guide and encourage the development of e-commerce.

要点概述

电子商务始于20世纪60年代，在90年代迅速发展，其启动和快速增长主要有以下因素：计算机的迅速发展和广泛应用；计算机处理速度和处理能力的逐步改善；应用范围越来越广泛；电子商务的应用促进了基础网络的普及和成熟；互联网安全、快速、低成本的特性和互联网用户的增长；电子支付方法的推广。电子支付方式因其方便、快速、安全等优势，解决了支付与结算的问题，从而形成了一个完善的全球网络支付与结算系统，同时，它还提供了一个在电子商务网络支付的重要手段。由于政府的支持和推动，电子商务受到政府和法律的重视，许多政府都出台了配套政策来引导和鼓励电子商务的发展。

With the Internet's characteristic of timely communication, manufacturers can dynamically price products according to their needs, thus ending the situation of national unified pricing and industry-recommended pricing, which will also lead to the disappearance of intermediaries, that is, non-intermediation. The fierce competition caused by e-commerce, the decrease of middlemen and the low transaction cost will make the brand cease to exist, and also eliminate the possibility of monopoly profits based on the brand, geographical location and exclusive access to production factors. The price of services and products will drop to a certain point at which the price is just equal to the cost of production plus the profitability of the capital market. Coupled with the small efforts of entrepreneurs, the unfair competitive advantage that brings huge benefits to investment capital will no longer exist. This is the vision of the first generation of e-commerce: frictionless business.

要点概述

有了Internet及时沟通的特性，生产商可以根据需求对产品动态定价，从而结束了全国统一定价和行业建议定价的局面，这也将导致中间商的消失，即非居间化。电子商务所导致的激烈竞争、中间商减少和低廉的交易成本将会使品牌不复存在，同时也消除了建立在品牌、地理位置、生产要素专有获取渠道专权上的垄断利润产生的可能性。服务和产品价格将下降到某一点，在这一点上，价格刚好等于生产成本加上资本市场盈利率，加上创业者的努力，给投资资本带来巨大收益的不公平竞争优势将不复存在，这是第一代电子商务的愿景——无摩擦商务。

1.4.2 Development process of global e-commerce

From the generation and development of EDI technology to today, the development of global e-commerce can be basically divided into four stages: brewing start, rapid expansion, difficult development and steady development.

要点概述

从 EDI 技术产生并开始发展一直到今天，全球电子商务的发展历程基本可以分为酝酿起步、急速扩张、艰难发展和稳步发展四个阶段。

EDI is an acronym for electronic data interchange in English. EDI refers to the standardization and formatting of commercial documents in accordance with agreed protocols, and the exchange and automatic processing of data between trading partners' computer network systems through computer networks, commonly known as "paperless trade".

要点概述

EDI 是英文 electronic data interchange 的缩写，可译为"电子数据交换"。EDI 是指按照商定的协议，将商业文件标准化和格式化，并通过计算机网络，在贸易伙伴的计算机网络系统之间进行数据交换和自动处理，俗称"无纸化贸易"。

1) Beginning stage of brewing

The origins of global e-commerce can be traced back to the 1970s. The development of EDI technology has attracted the attention of many countries. In the late 1960s, some of the big companies in Western Europe and North America are starting to use electronic means for data, tables, etc. The exchange of information in their respective business documents between different countries and regional trading partners in accordance with the same recognized standard is the initial e-business model.

要点概述

1) 酝酿起步期

全球电子商务的起源，可以追溯到 20 世纪 70 年代。EDI 技术的开发引起许多国家的关注。在 20 世纪 60 年代末，西欧和北美的一些大企业开始使用电子方式进行数据、表格等信息的交换，在不同国家和地域的贸易伙伴之间将各自的业务文件按照同一个公认的标准依靠计算机直接传递对方所需的信息，这就是最初的电子商务模式——电子数据交换。

From the beginning of EDI, it was applied to the transfer of drawings, documents, etc. between different departments within the company. Since no other manual rewriting is required in this process, the error rate is greatly reduced and the cost is saved. In the 1990s, EDI e-commerce technology was relatively mature, and the scope of application gradually expanded to areas such as international trade and finance. Even in the trade community, the slogan "No order without EDI" was put forward. In 1996, only the relevant companies in the United States generated $500 billion in corporate trade through EDI.

要点概述

从 EDI 出现开始，一开始是应用于企业内部不同部门之间传送图纸、文件等，由于在这一过程当中并不需要任何其他手动的改写等，从而大大降低了出错率，也为企业节省了成本。到了 20 世纪 90 年代，EDI 电子商务技术已经较为成熟，并且应用的范围逐渐扩大到国际贸易和金融等领域。甚至在贸易界提出了“没有 EDI 就没有订单”的口号，仅 1996 年全美各有关公司就通过 EDI 方式产生了 5000 亿美元的企业贸易额。

However, with the development of technology and the deepening of the application of EDI technology, people have gradually found that EDI has very high requirements for technology, equipment and personnel. The price is expensive so that it can only exist in advanced countries and regions. If this kind of malpractice cannot be solved, then this technology cannot be promoted and further developed in the world, which to a certain extent also restricts the trade export of developed countries to developing countries.

要点概述

但是，随着技术的发展和 EDI 技术应用的愈加深入，人们逐渐发现 EDI 对技术、设备、人员都有着非常高的要求，而且价格的昂贵使其仅仅能够在先进国家和地区中存在。这种弊端如果不能够得到解决，那么这项技术就不能在世界范围内得到推广和进一步的发展，这在一定程度上也制约了发达国家向发展中国家进行贸易出口。

In addition to the high efficiency and high accuracy of EDI, its advantages in business strategy are also outstanding. EDI can shorten the cycle of improving products or launching new products, and quickly gain more investment partner information to expand into new areas or markets. At the same time, EDI can effectively transform the business model from supply-driven to demand-led, save paper costs and reduce carbon emissions, thereby strengthening corporation's social responsibility and sustainability.

要点概述

除了 EDI 高效和准确率高的特点之外，其在商业运营的策略方面的优点也很突出。EDI 能够缩短改良产品或推出新产品的周期，快速获取更多投资伙伴信息以拓展新领域或市场。与此同时，EDI 还能有效地把商业模式由供应主导转化为由需求主导，并节约纸质成本，减少碳排放，从而加强企业的社会责任感及可持续性。

2) Stage of rapid expansion

With the breakthrough of network, communication and information technology, the Internet has exploded and rapidly spread around the world, giving modern business three characteristics of increasing supply capacity, customer demand and global competition. Under this new trend, a new business model based on the Internet, with both parties as the mainstay, with electronic payment and settlement of banks as the means, relying on customer data, that is, the e-commerce model emerged and rose. Since the 1990s, e-commerce has begun to abandon the era of relying solely on EDI technology. Internet-based e-commerce has received great attention and has begun to develop rapidly. In 1994, the world's first Internet shopping mall emerged, and the establishment of the center immediately attracted 34 stores. In 1995, in Swindon, England, the National Bank of Westminster, Midland Bank and British Telecom began experimenting with an electronic payment called Mondex to make online payments. With the birth of Amazon's online bookstore in July 1995, e-commerce began to become a hot spot for economic activities in various countries. A large amount of capital flowed into the e-commerce industry. E-commerce stocks and companies like Amazon Bookstore achieved rapid development at this stage. On 6 December 1996, the 85th plenary meeting of the United Nations adopted resolution 51/162, which formally promulgated *the UNCITRAL Model Law on Electronic Commerce and its Guide to Enactment* (the "Model Law on Electronic Commerce"). The promulgation of the "Model Law on Electronic Commerce" has regulated various behaviors in e-commerce activities and provided a model for e-commerce legislation in various countries, which greatly promoted the development of e-commerce in the world. In 2000, the volume of world e-commerce transactions reached $354.9 billion.

要点概述

2) 急速扩张期

随着网络、通信和信息技术的突破性进展，Internet 在全球爆炸式增长并迅速普及，使得现代商业具有不断增长的供货能力、客户需求和全球竞争三大特征。在这一新趋势下，一种基于互联网、以交易双方为主体、以银行电子支付和结算为手段、以客户数据为依托的全新商务模式，即电子商务模式出现并崛起。进入 20 世纪 90 年代以来，电子商务开始抛弃过去单纯依赖 EDI 技术的时代，基于 Internet 的电子商务受到了高度重视，并且开始快速发展起来。1994 年，出现了世界上第一个互联网购物中心，该中心的成立立刻吸引了 34 家商店进入。1995 年，在英国斯温登城，英国威斯敏斯特国民银行、米德兰银行和英国电信公司开始实验使用一种叫做 Mondex 的电子货币，实现了网上支付。随着 1995 年 7 月亚马逊网络书店的诞生，电子商务开始成为各国经济活动的热点，大量的资金流入电子商务行业，类似于亚马逊书店的电子商务股票和公司都在这一阶段实现了飞速发展。1996 年 12 月 6 日，联合国第 85 次全体会议通过了第 51/162 号决议，正式颁布了《贸易法委员会电子商业示范法及其颁布指南》（简称《电子商业示范法》）。《电子商业示范法》的颁布，规范了电子商务活动中的各种行为，为各国电子商务立法提供了一个范本，极大地促进了世界电子商务的发展。2000 年世界电子商务的交易额高达 3549 亿美元。

3) Difficult stage of development

With the rapid development in the late 1990s, the problem of e-commerce began to gradually emerge. At the beginning of the 21st century, the Internet economy was hit hard for the first time. The US Nasdaq index plummeted, and the shrinking value of online stocks made investors worried. For a time, much attention has focused on the Internet economy bubble. Those who know the stock market know the success of Nasdaq, the successful example of the world's second-tier market. In 2000, there were about 5,500 companies listed on the Nasdaq market, including Microsoft, Dell, Yahoo, Amazon and other world-class technology companies. On March 10, 2000, the Nasdaq market set a record of 5048.62 points, then reversed and continued to decline, and reached a record closing low of 1857.44 points on March 20. The collapse of the Nasdaq market is inseparable from the dot-com bubble. The "myth" created by Internet stocks such as Amazon and Yahoo has aroused the enthusiasm of investors at this point in time. The scale of the enterprise has grown too fast, and the production capacity of the products has greatly exceeded the actual demand of the market, resulting in an increase in inventories and a decrease in profits. More than one-third of the websites have disappeared.

要点概述

3) 艰难发展期

伴随着 20 世纪 90 年代末期的飞速发展，电子商务问题开始逐渐暴露出来。21 世纪初，因特网经济遭到第一次沉重打击。美国纳斯达克指数暴跌，网络股价值缩水使得投资人忧心忡忡。一时间，众多注意力聚焦于因特网经济泡沫。想必了解股市的人都知道纳斯达克这一世界二板市场发展的成功典范，2000 年，在纳斯达克市场上市的企业共有 5 500 家左右，其中包括了微软、戴尔、雅虎、亚马逊等世界级高科技企业。在 2000 年 3 月 10 日，纳斯达克市场曾经创下了 5 048.62 点的历史记录，随后逆转而下不断下滑，到 3 月 20 日又创下了历史收盘新低——1 857.44 点。这次纳克达斯市场的崩盘与网络泡沫是分不开的，之前以亚马逊、雅虎等网络股创造的“神话”在这一时间点激起了投资者的热情，投资的不断增长导致相关企业规模增长过快，产品的生产能力大大超过了市场的实际需求，导致库存增加，利润降低，超过 1/3 的网站销声匿迹了。

4) Stage of steady development

Faced with the grim situation of e-commerce development, relevant UN organizations have stepped up efforts in e-commerce development. On May 10, 2001, The United Nations Centre for Trade Facilitation and Electronic Business and Organization for the Advancement of Structured Information Standards formally approved the ebXML standard, which laid the foundation for expanding a unified global e-commerce transaction market. At the same time, governments have also introduced various incentive policies to continue to support the development of e-commerce. E-commerce has shaken off the impact of the IT industry bubble that triggered the shrinking world economy and entered a stage of steady development.

要点概述

4) 稳步发展期

面对电子商务发展的严峻形势，联合国有关组织加大了电子商务发展工作的力度。2001 年 5 月 10 日，联合国促进贸易和电子商务中心与结构化信息标准发展组织正式批准 ebXML 标准，为拓展一个统一的全球性电子商务交易市场奠定了基础。与此同时，各国政府也相继推出各种鼓励政策，继续支持电子商务的发展。电子商务摆脱了引发世界经济萎缩的 IT 行业泡沫影响，进入稳步发展阶段。

At this stage, not only large-scale companies and enterprises have adopted e-commerce, but many large-scale netizens have gradually accepted the way of online shopping as well. The B2B model has developed rapidly, and many small and medium-sized enterprises have also got a share of it. On this basis, the environment for the steady development of e-commerce is also constantly maturing, and the supporting logistics and payment issues have also been basically solved. E-commerce in the world has become splendid.

要点概述

在这个阶段，不仅仅是大型的公司、企业全面采用了电子商务，许多大批的网民也逐步接受了网络购物的方式，B2B 模式高速发展，许多中小型企业也从中分到了一杯羹。在这种基础上，电子商务稳步发展的环境也在不断地成熟，配套的物流、支付等问题也都得到了基本解决，全球范围内的电子商务变得异彩纷呈。

Notes:

1. Mondex

Modex 是基于智能卡的一种系统，Mondex 卡的尺寸与标准 IC 卡一样，卡上有一个 8

位的微电脑记录与处理数据。Mondex 卡将电子货币贮存在卡上的微电脑内。可通过专用电话直接从用户的银行账户上接收电子现金。持卡人可在有 Mondex 刷卡器的任何商家消费。两个持卡人还可用电话在他们的 Mondex 卡之间转移现金。同时一张卡既可在在线环境下使用，又可在普通商店里使用。另一个优点是顾客在各类自动售货机上都能找开零钱。它以电子形式储备真正的现金，用户因担心卡的失窃不会在卡上存放大笔资金。而且 Mondex 卡没有信用卡延期结算的优点，它必须立即支付现金。

2. 纳斯达克指数

纳斯达克指数是反映纳斯达克证券市场行情变化的股票价格平均指数，基本指数为100。纳斯达克上市公司涵盖所有新技术行业，包括软件和计算机、电信、生物技术、零售和批发贸易等，它主要由美国的数百家发展最快的先进技术、电信和生物公司组成，包括微软、英特尔、美国在线、雅虎这些家喻户晓的高科技公司，因而成为美国“新经济”的代名词。

3. 戴尔

戴尔（Dell），总部位于美国得克萨斯州朗德罗克的世界五百强企业，由迈克尔·戴尔于1984 年创立。戴尔以生产、设计、销售家用以及办公室计算机而闻名，不过它同时也涉足高端电脑市场，生产与销售服务器、数据储存设备、网络设备等。戴尔公司于 1992 年进入《财富》杂志 500 家之列，戴尔因此成为其中最年轻的首席执行官。自 1995 年起，戴尔公司一直名列《财富》杂志评选的“最受仰慕的公司”，2001 年排名第 10 位，2011 年上升至第 6 位。

4. 亚马逊

亚马逊公司（Amazon），是美国最大的一家网络电子商务公司，位于华盛顿州的西雅图。它是网络上最早开始经营电子商务的公司之一，成立于 1995 年。亚马逊一开始只经营网络的书籍的销售业务，现在则扩及到了范围相当广的其他产品，已成为全球商品品种最多的网上零售商和全球第二大互联网企业，在公司名下，也包括了 AlexaInternet、a9、lab126、和互联网电影数据库（Internet Movie Database，IMDB）等子公司。

5. ebXML

ebXML 是一组支持模块化电子商务框架的规范。ebXML 支持一个全球化的电子市场，它使得任意规模的企业通过交换基于 XML 的信息，能够不受地域限制地接洽和处理生意。ebXML 是联合国（UN/CEFACT，贸易促进和电子商务中心）和 OASIS（结构化信息标准发展组织）共同倡导、全球参与开发和使用的规范。最初因为 EDI 高昂的启动费用使得只有少部分企业能够使用，为了寻找一种使全球不同规模的公司都能受益的简单、便宜的交换标准商务文档的方法，最终发明了 ebXML。

Review questions:

According to the topic of this chapter, briefly answer the following questions:

(1) What is called cross-border e-commerce?

(2) What are the characteristics of cross-border e-commerce?

(3) According to different classifications, what types of E-commerce can be classified?

(4) Combine with reality, talk about the influence of the development of cross-border e-commerce on foreign trade.

(5) Briefly introduce the current situation of China's cross-border ecommerce development.

Chapter 2
Overview of Cross-border E-commerce

2.1 The definition of cross-border e-commerce

E-commerce generally refers to a new type of business operation mode based on browser/server application in an open Internet environment in a wide range of commercial trade activities around the world. In this model, buyers and sellers do not face each other with various business activities, but conduct online shopping for consumers, online transactions between merchants and online electronic payments, as well as various business activities, trading activities, financial activities and related comprehensive service activities.

These transactions most frequently involve the purchase or sale of goods and services ordered electronically, but the payment and delivery of goods or services may be performed in any form (outside the network). The most popular way to conduct these transactions is through the Internet, hence the name e-commerce.

要点概述

电子商务通常是指在全球各地广泛的商业贸易活动中，在因特网开放的网络环境下，基于浏览器/服务器应用方式，买卖双方不谋面地进行各种商贸活动，实现消费者的网上购物、商户之间的网上交易和在线电子支付以及各种商务活动、交易活动、金融活动和相关的综合服务活动的一种新型的商业运营模式。这些交易频繁地涉及以电子方式订购的商品和服务，但货物或服务的支付和交付可能以任何形式（也在网络之外）执行。

执行这些交易最流行的方法是通过互联网进行，因此得名电子商务。

电子商务的特点是没有国界，这是因为消费者可以通过互联网在世界上最偏远的角落进行购物。虽然大多数网上购物的顾客仍然会选择国内的网上商店，但是从国外的商店购买的商品越来越受欢迎，这就是所谓的跨境电子商务。

E-commerce is characterized by no borders because consumers can shop in the most remote corners of the world via the Internet. Although most online shoppers still choose domestic online stores, goods purchased from foreign stores are becoming more and more popular. This is called cross-border e-commerce.

要点概述

电子商务的特点是没有国界，这是因为消费者可以通过互联网在世界上最偏远的角落进行购物。虽然大多数网上购物的顾客仍然会选择国内的网上商店，但是国外商店的商品越来越受欢迎，这就是所谓的跨境电子商务。

Cross-border e-commerce refers to an international business activity in which transactions entities in different environments reach transactions through e-commerce platforms, perform payment settlement, and deliver goods through cross-border logistics. Last year, almost all EU member states of the e-commerce European organization pointed out that the share of cross-border e-commerce has increased, which proves that it will become one of the main factors driving the European and global e-commerce market.

要点概述

跨境电子商务是指分属不同环境的交易主体，通过电子商务平台达成交易、进行支付结算，并通过跨境物流送达商品、完成交易的一种国际商业活动。去年几乎所有电子商务欧洲组织的欧盟成员国都指出，跨境电子商务的份额有所增加，这证明它将成为推动欧洲和全球电子商务市场的主要因素之一。

Cross-border e-commerce is a more advanced form of e-commerce application, which means that both parties to the trade in different regions or countries can use the Internet or related information platforms to achieve this transaction. Cross-border e-commerce also has forms of e-commerce, such as B2C, B2B, C2C, etc.

要点概述

跨境电子商务是电子商务应用的更高级的形式，这意味着不同地区或国家的贸易双方都可以通过使用互联网或者相关信息平台来实现这一交易。跨境电子商务也有电子商务的形式，如 B2C、B2B、C2C 等。

2.2 The characteristic of cross-border e-commerce

1) Global Forum

The network is a medium without boundaries, with global and decentralized features. Cross-border e-commerce that is attached to the network is therefore characterized by global and decentralized nature.

要点概述

1）全球性

网络是一个没有边界的媒介，具有全球性和非中心化的特征，依附于网络发生的跨境电子商务也因此具有了全球性和非中心化的特性。

Cross-border e-commerce relies on e-commerce platforms for international trade, which determines the characteristics of its globalization. The global characteristics of cross-border e-commerce can maximize the sharing of information resources for sellers and buyers around the world, but there are also certain payment risks and settlement risks. Anyone who has mastered a certain basic knowledge of the network can enter information into the network and conduct online transactions whenever and wherever. However, due to cultural, political and legal differences, cross-border e-commerce also has many problems and uncertainties. The difficulty of taxation is also an important issue that hinders the further development of cross-border e-commerce.

要点概述

跨境电子商务以电子商务平台为依托进行国际贸易，决定了其全球化的特征。跨境电子商务的全球性特征能最大程度地给全球卖家和买家带来信息资源的共享，但同时也存在一定的支付风险和结算风险。任何人只要掌握了一定的网络基础知识，何时何地都可以将信息输入网络，进行网上交易。然而由于文化、政治和法律的不同，跨境电子商务也存在着许多问题和不确定性。税收方面的困难性也是阻碍跨境电子商务进一步发展的一个重要问题。

2) Intangible

Based on the characteristics of digital transmission activities, digital products and services are also intangible. In e-commerce, intangible products can replace physical objects to become transactions. A series of problems including how to define the nature of the transaction, how to supervise it, how to tax, and so on, has brought new issues to the tax and legal departments.

要点概述

2）无形性

数字化产品和服务基于数字传输活动的特性也必然具有无形性。在电子商务中，无形产品却可以替代实物成为交易的对象。而如何界定该交易的性质、如何监督、如何征税等一系列的问题却给税务和法律部门带来了新的课题。

3) Anonymous

Due to the decentralized and global nature of cross-border e-commerce, it is difficult to identify the identity of e-commerce users and their geographic location.

要点概述

3）匿名性

由于跨境电子商务的非中心化和全球性的特性，因此很难识别电子商务用户的身份和其所处的地理位置。

The anonymity of the network provides consumers with the convenience of allowing them to do so. The anonymity of cross-border e-commerce causes the extreme asymmetry of consumer rights and obligations. Consumers can enjoy the maximum rights and benefits in a virtual network environment, but they bear the minimum responsibilities and obligations, and some even try to avoid responsibility. This obviously brings endless difficulties to the tax collection of the state tax authorities. Because the parties to the transaction provide false information, they can't find the taxpayer's legal income tax by finding the trader's real income and trading situation, thus unable to calculate the tax payable and legally tax the taxpayer.

要点概述

网络的匿名性提供给消费者这样的便利条件，允许他们这样做。跨境电子商务的匿名性造成消费者权利与义务的极其不对称，消费者可以在虚拟的网络环境中享受最大的权利和利益，却承担最小的责任和义务，有的甚至想方设法逃避责任。这显然给国家税务机关征收税款带来了无尽的困难，因为交易双方提供虚假的信息，使得他们无法通过查找交易人获知真实的所得利益和交易情况，也就无法计算应缴税款，对纳税人进行合法征税。

4) Instantaneously

For the network, the speed of transmission is independent of geographic distance.

要点概述

4）即时性

对于网络而言，传输的速度和地理距离无关。

Different from the traditional foreign trade mode, cross-border e-commerce is instantaneous for the transmission of information, which means that no matter how far the actual geographical location is, the seller sends the information and the buyer receives the information almost simultaneously. This is equivalent to a face-to-face exchange of traditional foreign trade. The transactions, ordering, payment, delivery, and settlement of some digital goods (such as software, movies, etc.) can be completed instantaneously through the network, bringing great convenience to both parties.

要点概述

不同于传统对外贸易模式，跨境电子商务对于信息的传输是即时的，也就是说无论实际地理位置相距多远，卖家发送信息与买家接收信息几乎是同时进行的，不存在时间差，这在一定程度上等同于传统对外贸易的面对面交流磋商。对于一些数字化商品（如软件、电影等）的交易，下单、付款、交货、结算都可以通过网络瞬间完成，给交易双方带来极大的便利。

The immediacy of cross-border e-commerce reduces the middlemen's links in traditional foreign trade, allowing exporters to directly face the final consumer and improve the efficiency of trade, but it also hides the legal crisis.

要点概述

跨境电子商务的即时性特征减少了传统对外贸易中的中间商环节，使出口商直接面对最终消费者，提高了贸易的效率，但也隐藏了法律危机。

In the field of taxation, due to the immediacy of e-commerce activities, buyers and sellers can start, change and terminate trading activities at any time, increasing the arbitrariness of trade and reducing the effectiveness of trade. This made it impossible for the tax authorities to verify the true situation of the transactions between the two parties, the supervision invalid, and certain difficulties brought to the tax authorities.

要点概述

在税收领域表现为：由于电子商务活动的即时性，买卖双方可以随时开始、变动和终止交易活动，增加了贸易的随意性、降低了贸易的有效性。这使得税务机关无法查证双方交易的真实情况，监督无效，给税务机关征收税款带来了一定困难。

5) Paperless

In e-commerce, computer communication records replaced a series of paper transaction documents. The user sends or receives electronic information. Since electronic information exists and transmitted in the form of bits, the entire information transmission and reception process is paperless.

要点概述

5）无纸化

在电子商务中，计算机通信记录取代了一系列的纸面交易文件。用户发送或接收电子信息，由于电子信息以比特的形式存在和传送，信息的发送和接收过程实现了无纸化。

In e-commerce, transaction entities mainly use paperless operations, which is a typical feature of cross-border e-commerce unlike traditional trade. The seller sends information through the network, the buyer receives the information through the network, and the entire electronic information transmission process is paperless. On the one hand, paperless trading methods make information transmission free from the limitations of written documents, and are more efficient. On the other hand, it also causes confusion in the legal system. Because most of the current laws and regulations are based on "paper-based transactions", they are not suitable for "paperless" transactions in cross-border e-commerce. Cross-border e-commerce replaces written documents (such as written contracts, settlement documents, etc.) in traditional foreign trade with "paperless" trading. The tax authorities are unable to know the true situation of the taxpayer's transaction, which increases the difficulty for the tax authorities to obtain the taxpayer's operating status. It results in a large part of the tax loss, which is not conducive to the country's tax policy. In the "paperless" e-commerce environment, there is no legal contract and written evidence of material form, so the state's collection of stamp duty has no rules and regulations to follow.

要点概述

在电子商务中，交易主体主要使用无纸化的操作形式，这是跨境电子商务不同于传统贸易的典型特征。卖方通过网络发送信息，买方通过网络接收信息，整个电子信息的传输过程实现了无纸化。无纸化的交易方式一方面使信息传递摆脱书面文件的限制，更加有效率，另一方面也造成了法律制度的混乱。因为现行的法律法规多数是以"有纸交易"为出发点，并不适应跨境电子商务的"无纸化"交易。跨境电子商务以"无纸化"交易方式代替了传统对外贸易中的书面文件（如书面合同、结算单据等）进行贸易往来。税务机关无法获知纳税人交易的真实情况，增加了税务当局获取纳税人经营状况的难度，使得其中很大一部分税收流失，不利于国家的税收政策。在“无纸化”的电子商务环境下，没有物质形态的法律合同和书面凭证，因而国家对印花税的征收便无章可循，无法可依。跨境电子商务与传统国际贸易比较如表 2-1 所示。

表 2-1 跨境电子商务与传统国际贸易比较

差异	传统国际贸易	跨境电子商务
交易主体	企业 - 企业	企业 - 企业、企业 - 个人、个人 - 个人
交易环节	交易环节复杂，中间商多	交易环节简便，中间商少
运营成本	运营成本高	运营成本低
订单类型	大批量、小批次、周期长	小批量、多批次、周期短
贸易产品	类目少、更新慢	类目多、更新快
争端处理	完善	有待完善
通关结汇	传统、简便	缓慢、受限

2.3 The classification of cross-border e-commerce

(1) According to the direction of circulation of goods, it can be divided into import cross-border e-commerce and export cross-border e-commerce.

(2) According to the different transaction objects, it can be divided into B2B, B2C, C2C, B2G and B2B2C.

(3) According to different customs supervision methods, it can be divided into general cross-border e-commerce and bonded cross-border e-commerce.

(4) According to the different trading channels, it can be divided into EDI mode and Internet mode.

要点概述

（1）按照货物流通方向的不同，可以分为进口跨境电子商务和出口跨境电子商务。

（2）按照交易对象的不同，可以分为 B2B、B2C、C2C、B2G、B2B2C。

（3）按照海关监管方式的不同，可分为一般跨境电子商务和保税跨境电子商务。

（4）按照交易渠道的不同，可分为 EDI 方式和互联网方式。

2.4 The development present situation in China

Due to changes in international trade conditions, the growth rate of China's export trade has declined. Along with the rise of the "Internet +" economy, China's rapidly emerging cross-border e-commerce has begun to become a new trade method to hedge the decline in foreign trade growth. In 2016, China's cross-border e-commerce transactions totaled 6.5 trillion yuan, accounting for 31% of the country's total e-commerce transactions and 26% of total foreign trade. In cross-border e-commerce transactions, export e-commerce transaction volume accounted for the majority of 80%, reaching 520 million yuan. There are many cross-border e-commerce platforms in China with numerous giants. Among the main platforms for cross-border import, Netease oversea purchases account for one-fifth of the total market, and Tmall International, Vipshop International, and JD.com each shares an average of about 16%. According to the data of 2016, The transaction volume of cross-border e-commerce is relatively high in the policy-oriented provinces and the economically developed provinces. For the whole country, the development of cross-border e-commerce is uneven. There is little development in economically underdeveloped areas.

要点概述

由于国际贸易条件的变化，中国出口贸易增速有所下降。伴随着“互联网+”经济的兴起，中国迅速崛起的跨境电商开始成为对冲对外贸易增速下滑的贸易新方式。2016年，中国跨境电商交易总额达到6.5万亿元，占全国电商总交易额的31%，占对外贸易总额的比例达到了26%，在跨境电商交易额中，出口电商交易额占了主要部分，达到5.2亿元，占比80%。中国跨境电商平台众多，巨头林立。在跨境进口主要平台中，网易考拉海购占市场总额的五分之一，天猫国际、唯品国际、京东全球购平分秋色，各占16%左右。就全国而言，跨境电商发展不平衡，经济不发达地区基本没什么发展。

2.4.1 Market size

Under the national strategic background of "Belt and Road" and the Pilot Free Trade Zone, as an emerging country of e-commerce, China's activity of cross-border e-commerce continues to increase. According to the data in 2013, there are more than 200,000 foreign trade enterprises engaged in cross-border e-commerce and more than 5,000 cross-border e-commerce platform enterprises. In the short period of 7 years from 2008 to

2015, the market size of the e-commerce industry has quadrupled, from 3.2 trillion yuan in 2008 to 15.8 trillion yuan in 2015. The proportion of e-commerce market share of cross-border e-commerce has gradually increased. In 2008, this proportion was 25%, and by 2015 it was 34.2% (as shown in Figure 2–1).

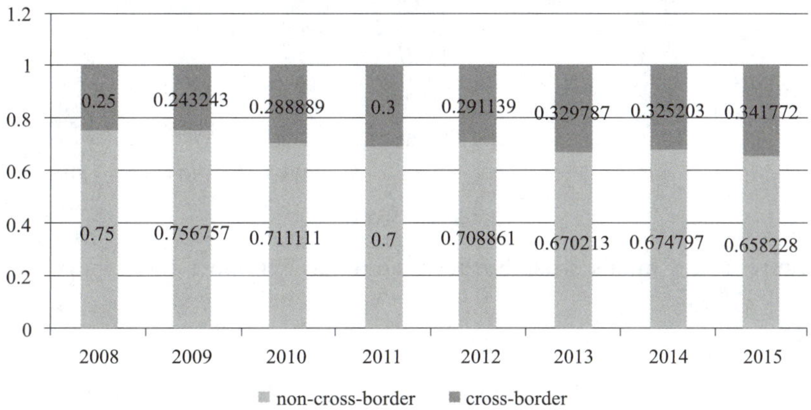

Figure 2–1 The market share proportion of cross-border e-commerce in e-commerce during 2008-2015

要点概述

在“一带一路”及自贸试验区等国家战略背景下，作为电子商务新兴国家，中国跨境电子商务市场活跃度持续提升。2013 年数据显示，中国开展跨境电子商务的外贸企业已超过 20 万家，跨境电子商务平台企业超过 5000 家。2008—2015 短短 7 年时间，电商行业市场规模翻了两番，从 2008 年的 3.2 万亿元增加到 2015 年的 15.8 万亿元。跨境电商的电商市场份额占比逐步攀升，2008 年该比重为 25%，2015 年则达到 34.2%，如表 2–1 所示。

2.4.2 Scale structure

From the distribution of cross-border e-commerce import and export structure, in 2014, cross-border e-commerce exports accounted for 86.7% and imports 13.3% (as shown in Figure 2–2).The proportion of imported e-commerce was low. However, with the opening of China's cross-border online shopping market, the improvement of the cross-border online shopping infrastructure and the development of consumers' cross-border online shopping habits, the proportion of imported e-commerce will gradually increase in the future.

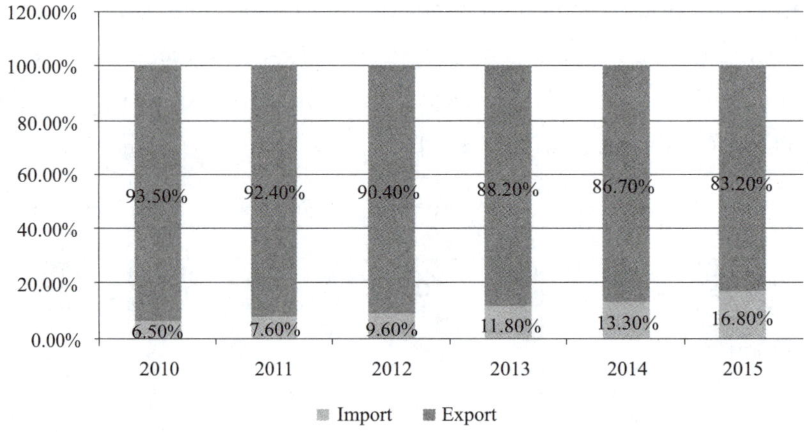

Figure 2–2 China's cross-border e-commerce' import and export ratio

要点概述

从跨境电商进、出口结构分布情况来看，2014 年跨境电商的出口占达到 86.7%，进口占比在 13.3%，如图 2–2 所示，进口电商比重较低，但随着中国跨境网购市场的开放、跨境网购基础环境的完善以及消费者跨境网购习惯的养成，未来进口电商比重将逐步增大。

2.4.3 Target market

Europe, North America and Japan are the main markets for cross-border e-commerce in China. Since the second half of 2011, the demand for e-commerce procurement from China in Russia, Brazil, India and Southeast Asia has grown rapidly. Among them, the United States and the European Union account for a large proportion, followed by the Asian regions around China, such as ASEAN, Japan, South Korea, India and Russia. The average annual growth rate of the United States, the United Kingdom, Germany and Australia is about 15%, 16%, 21% and 8%, and the transaction amount will reach 98.1 billion yuan, 15.5 billion yuan, 13.4 billion yuan and 5.6 billion yuan respectively. As the representative of emerging markets, Brazil has the largest growth rate. Looking at the cross-border e-commerce export flow, the target market of cross-border e-commerce in China is relatively concentrated.

要点概述

欧洲、北美及日本是中国跨境电子商务的主要市场。从 2011 年下半年开始，俄罗斯、巴西、印度、东南亚国家对中国的电子商务采购需求快速增长。其中，美国和欧盟所占比重较大，其次主要流向中国周边的亚洲地区，如东盟、日本、韩国、印度和俄罗斯等。美国、英国、德国和澳大利亚每年平均增长率约为 15%、16%、21% 和 8%，交易金额将分别达到 981 亿元、155 亿元、134 亿元和 56 亿元。巴西作为新兴市场的代表，增速最大。以跨境电子商务出口流向地来看，中国跨境电商的目标市场相对集中，2008—2015 年中国跨境电商占电商市场份额如图 2-3 所示。

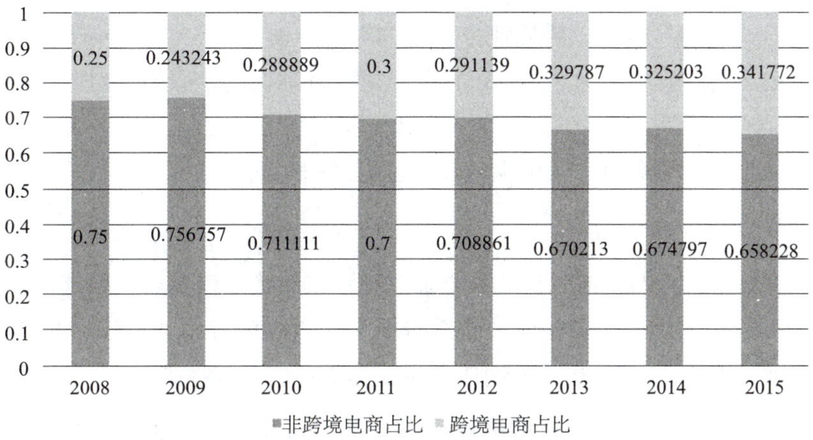

图 2-3　2008—2015 年中国跨境电商占电商市场份额

Notes:

1. 印花税

印花税是对经济活动和经济交往中书立、领受具有法律效力凭证的行为所征收的一种税。因采用在应税凭证上粘贴印花税票作为完税的标志而得名。印花税的纳税人包括在中国境内设立、领受规定的经济凭证的企业、行政单位、事业单位、军事单位、社会团体、其他单位、个体工商户和其他个人。

2. B2G

B2G 模式即企业与政府之间通过网络所进行的交易活动的运作模式，比如电子通关，电子报税等。B2G 比较典型的例子是网上采购，即政府机构在网上进行产品，服务的招标和采购。这种运作模式的优势是投标费用降低，因为供货商可以直接从网上下载招标书，并以电子数据的形式发回投标书。与此同时，供货商可以得到更多的甚至是世界范围内的投标机会。由于通过网络进行投标，即使是规模较小的公司也能获得投标的机会。

3. B2B2C

所谓 B2B2C 是一种新型网络通信销售方式，是英文“business to business to Customer”的简称。其中第一个 B 指广义的卖方（即成品、半成品、材料提供商等），第二个 B 指交易平台，即提供卖方与买方的联系平台，平台同时提供优质的附加服务，C 即指买方。在这三者中，卖方不仅仅是公司，也包括个人，即一种逻辑上的买卖关系中的卖方。平台也并非是简单的中介，而是能够提供高附加值服务的渠道机构，并且是拥有客户管理、信息反馈、数据库管理、决策支持等功能的服务平台。买方同样是逻辑上的关系，可以是内部也可以是外部的。B2B2C 定义包括了现存的 B2C 和 C2C 平台的商业模式，使其更加综合化，可以提供更优质的服务。

4. 网易考拉海购

网易考拉海购是网易旗下以跨境业务为主的综合型电商，于 2015 年 1 月 9 日公测，销售品类涵盖母婴、美容彩妆、家居生活、营养保健、环球美食、服饰箱包、数码家电等。网易考拉海购以 100% 正品、天天低价、7 天无忧退货、快捷配送服务为宗旨，为消费者提供了海量海外商品，希望使用户“用更少的钱，过更好的生活”。

5. 京东

京东是中国自营式电商企业，创始人刘强东担任京东集团董事局主席兼首席执行官。旗下设有京东商城、京东金融、拍拍网、京东智能、O2O 及海外事业部等。2013 年正式获得虚拟运营商牌照。2014 年 5 月在美国纳斯达克证券交易所正式挂牌上市。2016 年 6 月与沃尔玛达成深度战略合作，1 号店并入京东。

6. 一带一路

“一带一路”是“丝绸之路经济带”和“21 世纪海上丝绸之路”的简称，2013 年 9 月和 10 月，中国国家主席习近平分别提出建设“新丝绸之路经济带”和“21 世纪海上丝绸之路”的合作倡议。它将充分依靠中国与有关国家既有的双多边机制，并借助既有的、行之有效的区域合作平台。一带一路旨在借用古代丝绸之路的历史符号，高举和平发展的旗帜，积极发展与沿线国家的经济合作伙伴关系，共同打造政治互信、经济融合、文化包容的利益共同体、命运共同体和责任共同体。

Review questions:

According to the topic of this chapter, briefly answer the following questions:

(1) What is called cross-border e-commerce?

(2) What are the characteristics of cross-border e-commerce?

(3) According to different classifications, what types of E-commerce can be classified?

(4) Combine with reality, talk about the influence of the development of cross-border e-commerce on foreign trade.

(5) Briefly introduce the current situation of China’s cross-border ecommerce development.

Chapter 3
Operating Mode

3.1 Graphic of operating mode

E-commerce is one of the most dynamic and important sectors of the economy. The latest trend in this market is cross-border trade based on selling products to customers in other countries. However, this is related to several issues, such as high costs, long-term delivery, language barriers and different legal and tax conditions. Cross-border e-commerce companies can directly cooperate with third-party integrated service platforms to them to conduct logistics, customs clearance and other links to complete the entire cross-border e-commerce transaction process.

要点概述

电子商务是经济中最具活力和最重要的部门之一。这一市场的最新趋势是基于向其他国家的客户销售产品的跨境贸易。然而这与几个问题有联系，如高成本、长期交货、语言障碍、不同的法律和税务条件等。跨境电商企业或直接与第三方综合服务平台合作，让第三方综合服务平台代办物流、通关商检等一系列环节，从而完成整个跨境电商交易的过程，跨境电子商务运营方式如图 3–1 所示。

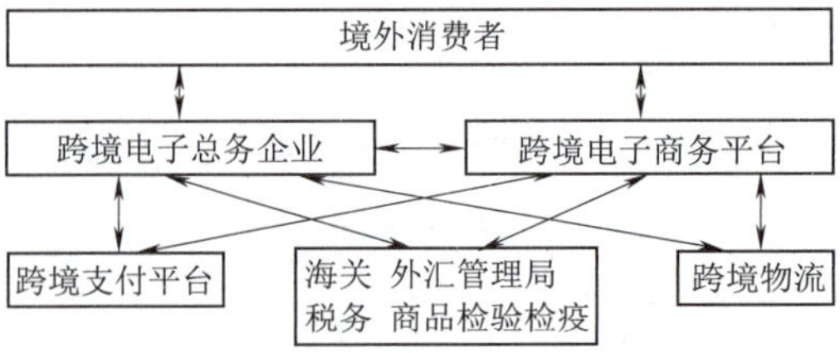

图 3-1　跨境电子商务运营方式

3.2 The characteristics of operating mode

3.2.1 Deepen of the electric business industry

The cross-border e-commerce operation mode of value-added chain service has developed from the e-commerce platform to the cross-border e-commerce operation mode. The value-added service of the industry chain has been deepened and developed into a comprehensive cross-border e-commerce trading environment including transaction, payment, logistics and quality assurance, which provides a relatively complete service in logistics transportation, customs clearance inspection, tax refund settlement, and forms a very mature industrial chain integrating transaction, logistics, finance, marketing and risk control.

要点概述

增值链服务跨境电商运营模式从开始的电商平台发展到跨境电商代运营模式，其产业链增值服务不断深化，发展成一个包含交易、支付、物流以及质量保障的综合性跨境电商交易环境，在物流运输、通关检验、退税结汇方面提供一个比较完善的服务，形成一套非常成熟的集交易、物流、金融、营销、风险控制等为一体的成熟产业链。

3.2.2 Integrated marketing

The process of SMEs applying cross-border e-commerce to overseas expansion has experienced a process of lack of information and information flooding. Traditional overseas marketing methods such as international exhibitions, electronic samples, industry magazines and email marketing are no longer suitable for the era of e-commerce development. The essence of integrated marketing lies in the integration and application of multi-channel and multi-resources, aiming at diversifying information. Buyers can find foreign trade enterprises through channels such as Google and Yahoo search engines to realize the integration and aggregation of multi-channel resources, so that China's foreign trade enterprises can obtain first-hand foreign buyers' enquiries. In addition to information integration, cross-border e-commerce integrates more social marketing elements, including blog marketing, SNS social marketing, etc. By integrating rich and high-quality resources, China's export enterprises will gain more exposure and business opportunities.

要点概述

中小企业应用跨境电商实现海外拓展过程中，经历了信息缺乏到信息泛滥的过程。国际展会、电子样本、行业杂志以及邮件营销等这些传统的海外营销方式不再适合电商发展的时代，整合营销的精髓在于多渠道和多资源的整合和运用，旨在进行信息多元化，让买家通过搜索引擎等渠道找到外贸企业，实现多渠道资源的整合和聚合，让中国的外贸企业获得一手的国外买家询盘。除了进行信息整合，跨境电商融合了更多的社会化营销元素，包括 SNS 社会化营销等，通过整合丰富优质资源，中国出口企业会获得更多的曝光和商机。

3.2.3 Basis of large data

Cross-border e-commerce is supported by big data. Cross-border e-commerce is based on Internet thinking. Both parties to the transaction reach a transaction through an online platform, so the platform has a very rich data base, a large amount and a wide variety. Many cross-border platforms are tailor-made for SMEs, and they have launched big data tools to conduct data analysis and research to provide decision-making basis for the marketing and development of enterprises. For example, Google's Google Analytics tool can provide marketing data such as lost customer analysis, natural traffic, buyer analysis, etc. of the seller's own store, as well as detailed data analysis such as the distribution of transaction attributes and soaring treasures of the industry. Alibaba AliExpress's "data aspect" analysis tool helps sellers analyze their own store data and huge industry data. Aodao China implements marketing data analysis, SEO data detection and analysis, and statistical analysis of website access data.

要点概述

跨境电商以大数据为支撑。跨境电商基于互联网思维，交易双方通过在线平台沟通达成交易，因此平台拥有非常丰富的数据基础，量大且数据类型繁多。很多跨境平台为中小企业量身制作，纷纷推出大数据工具，开展数据分析和研究，为企业的营销和发展提供决策依据。比如谷歌推出的谷歌分析工具，能提供卖家自己店铺的流失顾客分析、自然流量、买家分析等营销数据，还可以查询店铺所属行业的成交属性分布、飙升宝贝等详尽的数据分析。阿里巴巴速卖通推出的“数据纵横”分析工具，帮助卖家分析自己店铺的相关数据以及庞大的行业数据。奥道中国实行营销数据分析、SEO 数据检测分析、网站访问数据统计分析。

Big data is now crucial for cross-border e-commerce. E-commerce can effectively improve the efficiency and sales volume by analyzing the interest of customers more rationally by pushing products that meet the psychological needs of customers.

要点概述

大数据在如今对于跨境电商来说是至关重要的，电商还能够通过对客户的兴趣的分析更合理地推送符合客户心理需求的产品，从而有效地提高了效率和销售量。

3.3 The operating mode of foreign trade imports and foreign trade exports

Cross-border e-commerce includes foreign trade exports and foreign trade imports.

要点概述

跨境电子商务包括外贸出口和外贸进口。

3.3.1 Foreign trade imports

Imported cross-border e-commerce operation mode is to establish foreign trade import network Purchase platform. With the liberalization of the FTA policy and the pilot of the electronic trade clearance policy, the import of cross-border electric*business gradually began to become a hot spot in the industry since 2016. The traditional primary form of the import of cross-border electric power suppliers is Haitao.com.

要点概述

进口跨境电子商务运营模式是建立外贸进口网络采购平台。随着自贸协定政策的放开和电子通关政策的试点，2016 年以来跨境电商进口逐渐成为行业热点。传统跨境电商进口的主要形式是海淘网。

Cross-border import e-commerce can be divided into platform type B2C, self-operated type B2C, and buyer type C2C according to different transaction entities. Platform type

B2C refers to the e-commerce provider to provide trading platform. The seller enters the platform. The platform provides services such as display, sales and payment for the merchant. It does not purchase and transport itself. The platform profit source is mainly commission and advertising expenses. The platform type B2C representatives are Tmall International and JD.com. Tmall International is a pure platform model while JD.com Global Purchase is a platform plus self-operated model. The self-operated B2C operating model requires full involvement in the operation of the entire supply chain. Its main source of profit is the commodity price difference. It is represented by Netease koala, Vipshop International, Jumei Premium. In the C2C mode of operation, after the customer places an order, the overseas buyer buys the goods and delivers them to the customer through international logistics. At present, there are few domestic C2C e-commerce platforms, represented by Alibaba's ocean terminal and Taobao global purchase.

要点概述

跨境进口电商按交易主体不同可分为平台型 B2C，自营型 B2C，买手型 C2C。平台型 B2C 是指电商提供交易平台，卖家进驻平台，平台为商家提供展示、销售、支付等服务，自身不进行采购和运输，平台利润来源主要为佣金和广告费用。平台型 B2C 代表有天猫国际、京东全球购，其中天猫国际是纯平台模式，京东全球购是平台加自营模式。自营型 B2C 运营模式需要全面介入整个供应链的运作，主要利润来源为商品差价。代表有网易考拉海购、唯品国际、聚美优品等。C2C 运作模式为客户下单后，海外买手购买商品，通过国际物流运送给客户，目前国内 C2C 电商平台较少，代表有阿里巴巴旗下的洋码头、淘宝全球购。

However, in the 2014, the former Haitao.com and other terms will be imported into the concept of cross-border electric business redefined.

要点概述

但在 2014 年，之前的海淘网等术语将被引入跨境电商概念重新界定。

3.3.2 Foreign trade exports

The cross-border e-commerce of foreign trade export is divided into the following several modes of operation:

(1) with the help of local foreign trade e-commerce platform. Its value chain form: Suppliers of export commodities, cross-border e-commerce platform, overseas consumers. In this model, the platform builds an IT architecture, transforms itself into an operations center, aggregates suppliers and consumers, forms economies of scale, provides marketing,

and the products are uploaded and supplied by suppliers.

(2) The use of foreign well-known e-commerce platforms.

(3) Seeking foreign shop shopping for the distribution of goods.

(4) Foreign trade enterprises from the construction of Cross-border Electronic Business Service system facing overseas market directly.

要点概述

外贸出口的跨境电子商务分为如下几种运营方式：

（1）借助本土的外贸电子商务平台。其价值链形态为：出口商品的供应商—跨境电子商务平台—境外消费者。在这种模式中，平台搭建 IT 架构，将自己打造成运营中心，聚集供应商和消费者，形成规模效应，负责营销推广，产品由供应商上传和供货。

（2）借助国外知名电子商务平台。

（3）寻求国外网店代购分销商品。

（4）外贸企业自建跨境电子商务系统直接面向海外市场。2005—2015 年中国进出口贸易和增长率变化情况如图 3-2 所示。

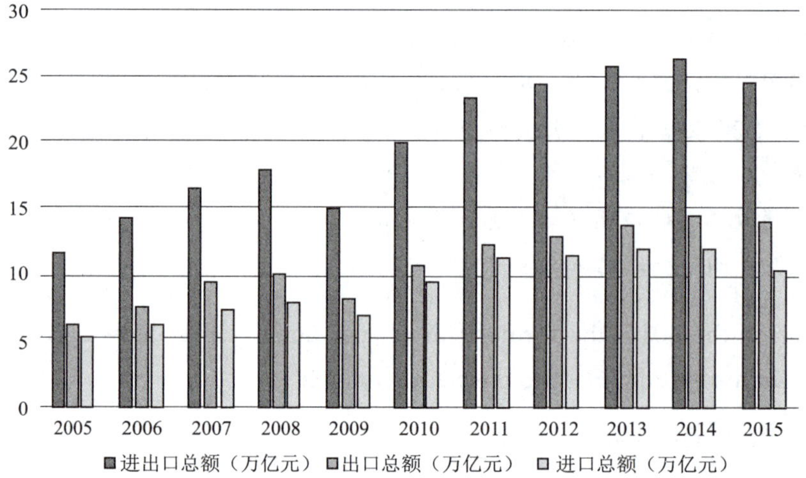

图 3-2　2005—2015 年中国进出口贸易和增长率变化情况

3.4 The process of operation

3.4.1 Logistics

In the case of self-operated e-commerce companies like Jingdong, when the e-commerce platform releases product information, these goods are already in the logistics distribution center. After the purchaser makes a purchase decision, the goods are handed over from the place of storage to the logistics company (carrier), and the carrier is responsible for transporting the goods from domestic to foreign shoppers. Jingdong, with independent logistics, has its own advantages in transportation. Such services as limited time delivery, next-day delivery, extremely fast delivery, and jingzhunda are available to Jingdong.

要点概述

就类似于京东自营这样的电商来说，在电商平台发布商品信息时，这些商品已经在物流集散中心；购物者在做出购买决策后，商品即从其存放地交由物流企业（承运人），承运人接受委托后负责将商品由国内运往国外购物者手中。有独立物流的京东在运输方面有着自己的优势，211 限时达、次日达、极速达、京准达等都是京东可以提供的服务。

3.4.2 Capital flows

To reduce transaction costs, cross-border electronic transactions are best settled electronically. Unlike domestic e-commerce, foreign shoppers can only pay their own currencies, but the sellers can only accept renminbi, and there is an exchange in the middle.

The status quo of cross-border e-commerce development is:

要点概述

为了降低交易成本，跨境电子交易最好以电子方式结算。与中国电子商务不同的是，外国购物者只能支付本国货币，而卖家只能接受人民币，中间有一个交易所。

跨境电子商务发展现状为：

1) The number of cross-border payment institutions has risen steadily

As of 2016, the People's Bank of China has issued payment licenses to 266 payment institutions. On this basis, the State Administration of Foreign Exchange issued a cross-border payment license to 30 of them, allowing them to conduct cross-border payment services.

要点概述

1）跨境支付机构数量稳中升

截至 2016 年，中国人民银行已经对 266 家支付机构颁发了支付牌照，在此基础上国家外汇管理局对其中 30 家支付机构颁发了跨境支付牌照，允许其开展跨境支付业务。

2) Rapid growth in cross-border payment transactions

According to statistics, in 2016, the total amount of cross-border e-commerce transactions worldwide has reached 13 trillion yuan. In 2016, China's cross-border e-commerce transactions reached 6.7 trillion yuan, accounting for 20% of China's total import and export trade, up 24% year-on-year.

要点概述

2）跨境支付交易额增长迅速

据统计，2016 年，全球范围内跨境电商交易总额已经达到 13 万亿元。2016 年中国跨境电商交易规模达 6.7 万亿元，占中国总进出口贸易额的 20%，同比增长 24%。

3) Accelerating the pace of cross-border payment overseas

With the technical achievements, operational capabilities and business experience accumulated in the development of the domestic market, various third-party payment platforms are accelerating the pace of global deployment. For example, Ant Financial Services Group, which belongs to Alipay, has settled in the United States, the United Kingdom, Thailand, India, Singapore and other countries, covering Asia, Europe, North America and other regions.

要点概述

3）跨境支付海外布局步伐加快

借助在国内市场发展中积累的技术成果、运营能力和业务经验，各第三方支付平台正在加快布局全球的步伐。例如，支付宝所属的蚂蚁金服集团已进驻美国、英国、泰国、印度、新加坡等国家，覆盖亚洲、欧洲、北美等地区。

4) Continuous expansion of cross-border payment services

At present, most of the payment agencies with cross-border payment licenses mainly carry out trade in goods, study abroad, air tickets and hotel accommodation. A small number of payment institutions provide tourism services, international exhibitions, international transportation, communication services, and software services. The business areas need to be further expanded and enriched.

要点概述

4）跨境支付业务不断拓展

目前，具有跨境支付牌照的支付机构中绝大部分主要开展的业务有货物贸易、留学教育、航空机票以及酒店住宿。少部分支付机构提供旅游服务、国际展览、国际运输、通信服务、软件服务，业务领域有待进一步拓展和丰富。

5) Strong momentum in cross-border mobile payment development

While the mobile payment scene is constantly enriched, the types of mobile payment products are also increasing to meet the needs of consumers.

要点概述

5）跨境移动支付发展势头强劲

在移动支付场景不断丰富的同时，为满足消费者的需求，移动支付产品的种类也在不断增加。

3.4.3 The flow of management

The whole process of cross-border electronic transactions is faced with the requirements of corresponding public administration, which mainly include the following aspects:

要点概述

跨境电子交易的整个过程都面临着相应公共管理的要求，主要包括以下几个方面：

The first is product quality inspection.

要点概述

一是产品质量检查。

The second is foreign exchange management, the process of paying the purchase price to the domestic seller by the foreign purchaser.

要点概述

二是外汇管理。货款由国外购买者向国内售卖者支付货款的过程。

The third is customs entry and exit management. When the products are exported, on the one hand, they need to accept the inspection and quarantine of the relevant departments. On the other hand, they need to accept customs clearance management and withhold customs duties.

要点概述

三是海关出入境管理。产品在出关时，一方面需要接受有关部门的产品检验检疫，另一方面需要接受海关部门的通关管理，扣缴关税。

The fourth is tax collection and tax refund. Products that are electronically traded by enterprises will pay taxes in all aspects according to the relevant laws and regulations of the state. When exporting, they can also receive tax rebate subsidies according to the relevant national industry promotion policies.

要点概述

四是税收征缴与退税。企业通过电子交易的产品会根据国家的有关法律法规缴纳各方面的税收，出口时还能根据国家相关产业促进政策而获得退税补贴。

Fifth, the problem of information asymmetry between buyers and sellers of cross-border e-commerce is more serious than that of domestic e-commerce. In the whole transaction process of cross-border e-commerce, on the one hand, cross-border buyers must pay the cross-border sellers after placing orders on the platform, but the seller's store merchandise display does not make the buyers really understand the product quality, and it is more difficult to make accurate judgments of the seller's credit and after-sales service levels; on the other hand, cross-border sellers are also difficult to predict and evaluate buyers' spending power and credit levels. Cross-border buyers mostly make international payments by credit card, but withdraw the payment after receiving the goods, or refuse to accept the goods for various reasons. Cross-border sellers therefore lose logistics costs and fees, and even money and goods. At present, Alibaba, eBay, Dunhuang Net, LightInTheBox and other platforms mainly use cross-border seller credit as a reference, lacking a scientific and feasible credit evaluation system. The construction of cross-border e-commerce credit system and institutional arrangements are urgently needed to be solved in the development of cross-border e-commerce.

要点概述

五是相对于中国电商，跨境电商买卖双方的信息不对称问题更为严重。在跨境电商的整个交易过程中，一方面，跨境买家在平台下单后须先付款给跨境卖家，但仅仅通过卖家店铺商品展示并不能使买家真正了解产品质量，更难对卖家信用以及售后服务水平做出准确判断；另一方面，跨境卖家也难以对买家的消费能力和信用水平做出预测和评价，跨境买家多通过信用卡完成国际支付，但却在收到货物后撤回支付，或以各种理由拒绝收货，跨境卖家损失物流费用和手续费，甚至钱货两空。目前阿里巴巴、eBay、敦煌网、兰亭集势等平台主要将跨境卖家信誉度作为参考，缺乏科学可行的信用评价体系，跨境电商信用体系建设和制度安排是跨境电商发展中急需解决的问题。

Sixth is the handling of cross-border transaction disputes. Domestic cross-border e-commerce is at a high-speed development stage, but many legal issues have also arisen. The original domestic international trade legal system has gradually failed to adapt to the current international e-commerce development environment. At the same time, the frequency of revision of the legal system related to China is far from being able to adapt to the development of cross-border e-commerce industry.

要点概述

六是跨境交易纠纷处理。中国跨境电子商务正处于高速发展阶段，但许多法律问题也随之而出，中国原有的国际贸易法律体系已逐渐不能适应当前国际电子商务发展的环境。同时，中国与之相关的法律制度修订频率也远远不能适应于跨境电商产业的发展。

Therefore, it is an urgent issue to develop a legal system that can adapt to current cross-border e-commerce to solve the institutional problems and legal disputes that may occur in e-commerce activities.

要点概述

因此，制定一套能够适应于当前跨境电子商务的法律体系是迫在眉睫的问题，只为能够解决当前在电子商务活动中可能发生的制度问题以及法律纠纷。

3.4.4 Information flow

All necessary processes of logistics, capital flow, and management flow must be transformed into information that is uniformly stored, transmitted, processed, and applied. After a certain logical processing, all of this information is integrated to form a complete electronic transaction information flow. Although the above four aspects of logistics, capital flow, management flow, and information flow are based on the situation that domestic online stores sell products to foreign consumers through domestic e-commerce platforms, other types of cross-border e-commerce and situation also exist. The various forms of cross-border e-commerce should include the flow of these four elements.

要点概述

物流、资金流、管理流的所有必要过程都必须能够转化为统一保存、传输、加工和应用的信息，经过一定的逻辑处理，所有这些信息整合起来即构成完整的电子交易信息流。虽然上述的物流、资金流、管理流、信息流等四个层面是基于中国网店通过中国电商平台向国外消费者销售产品的情况而展开的，但是对于跨境电子商务的其他各种类型、情况来说，也都是同样存在的。跨境电子商务的各种形式都应该包含这四个要素的流动。

Notes

1. 资金流

资金流（fund flow）就是指在营销渠道成员间随着商品实物及其所有权的转移而发生的资金往来流程。

2. 信息流

信息流有广义和狭义两种。广义指在空间和时间上向同一方向运动过程中的一组信息，它们有共同的信息源和信息的接收者，即由一个信息源向另一个单位传递的全部信息的集合。狭义指信息的传递运动，这种传递运动是在现代信息技术研究、发展、应用的条件中，信息按照一定要求通过一定渠道进行的。

3. FTA

自由贸易协定（free trade agreement），是两国或多国间具有法律约束力的契约，目的在于促进经济一体化，其目标之一是消除贸易壁垒，允许产品与服务在国家间自由流动。这里所指的贸易壁垒可能是关税，也可能是繁杂的规则等等。

4. 增值链

增值链是指企业为了创造更高的新增价值经过系统整合的全部增值环节。现代企业价值，由实体经济部分的价值链和虚拟经济部分的增值链构成。企业在运营的过程中要发展独特的竞争优势，要创造更高的新增价值，要实现系列的增值过程，要整合能够实现增值的各个环节，来完善企业的增值链。

5. SME

SME（small and medium enterprises），是中小型企业的意思，不同的国家对中小型企业的定义标准是不同的。例如，欧盟国家目前的标准是雇员少于 49 人的企业为小型企业，少于 249 人的是为中型企业。而在美国，雇员少于 99 人的企业为小型企业，少于 500 人的为中型企业。

6. 聚美优品

聚美优品是一家化妆品限时特卖商城，其前身为团美网，由陈欧、戴雨森等于 2010 年 3 月创立。聚美优品首创“化妆品团购”模式，即每天在网站推荐十几款热门化妆品。2010 年 9 月，团美网正式全面启用聚美优品新品牌，并且启用全新顶级域名。聚美优品于 2014 年 5 月 16 日在纽交所正式挂牌上市。

Review questions:

According to the topic of this chapter, briefly answer the following questions:

(1) Briefly explain the operating mode of cross-border electronic commerce.

(2) What are the characteristics of the cross-border electric business platform operating mode?

(3) How many aspects the requirements of corresponding public administration which cross-border e-commerce faced mainly include?

(4) What elements should be involved in the various forms of Cross-border e-commerce?

Chapter 4

Business Model of Cross-border E-commerce

4.1 Development status

Cross-border e-commerce has developed rapidly in recent years, with the advent of network technology and new traffic, a variety of business models has emerged. The current mainstream of cross-border e-commerce models mainly includes B2C,B2B,C2C,C2B,BMC.

要点概述

近年来，跨境电子商务发展迅速，随着网络技术的出现和新流量的出现，各种商业模式应运而生。目前跨境电商主流模式主要有 B2C、B2B、C2C、C2B、BMC。

4.2 Business model

Electronic commerce generally refers to the use of the Internet (or proprietary intranets) to conduct commercial activities of various kinds, and as mentioned above it can be partitioned into B2B and B2C (or electronic retailing) segments. With respect to the B2C segment, a relevant term that has previously appeared in the academic literature is teleshopping. Teleshopping refers to the use of ICT to obtain information about or purchase consumer goods: pre-internet services such as home-shopping channels on cable television, specialized early computer-based systems such as the Minitel in France, and even telephone orders from a catalog mailed to the home can be placed in this category. Thus, e-shopping basically refers to the B2C segment of e-commerce, but with a focus on the set of activities shopping that are undertaken by the consumer.

要点概述

电子商务一般是指利用 Internet 或专有内部网进行各种各样的商业活动，如上所述，它可以分为（B2B）和（B2C）两部分。关于 B2C 部分，之前在学术文献中出现的一个相关术语是电话购物。电话购物是指利用 ICT 获取信息或购买消费品。互联网服务，如家庭购物频道有线电视、专业早期的计算机系统，如 Minitel 在法国，甚至电话订单目录寄给家里可以放在这一类。因此，电子购物基本上是指电子商务的 B2C 环节，但重点是消费者进行的购物活动的集合。

In the United States, Japan, South Korea and other countries, TV shopping is an important channel for consumers to purchase goods. In this way, merchants continue to provide high-quality products and distribution services to the vast number of consumers in front of the TV. Sales of US cable TV alone amounted to tens of billions of dollars a year. Among them, TV shopping company QVC was established in 1986. In 1987, its operating income was only over 100 million US dollars, and by 2006 it had grown to 8 billion US dollars.

要点概述

在美国、日本、韩国等国家，电视购物都是消费者购买商品的一个重要渠道，商家通过这种方式，向电视机前的广大消费者源源不断地提供着优质的产品以及配送服务。仅美国有线电视网电视购物一年的销售额就达上百亿美元。其中，电视购物公司 QVC 成立于 1986 年，在 1987 年的营业收入仅有 1 亿多美元，而到 2006 年已增长到 80 亿美元。

4.2.1 Business to customer

“Business-to-customer” (B2C) is a model of e-commerce, which is a business retail model that directly sells products and services to consumers. It attracts consumers by using economies of scale, and then lowers prices to increase profits.

要点概述

B2C 是一种电子商务模式，它是一种直接向消费者销售产品和服务的商业零售模式。它利用规模经济来吸引消费者，然后降低价格以增加利润。

In the B2B transaction, the seller's Enterprise sells personal consumer goods on the e-commerce platform, the trade object is the foreign consumer, it takes the air parcel, the courier, the mail as the logistics means, it takes express or the postal company as the declaration main body.

要点概述

在B2B交易中，卖方企业在电子商务平台上销售个人消费品，交易对象为外国消费者，以航空包裹、快递、邮件为物流方式，以快递或邮政公司为报关主体。

Indications are that e-commerce, in some form and at some level, is here to stay in many contexts it is quite clearly superior to the old way of doing business. To urban planners, then, the impact of e-commerce on transportation is a relevant question. Although the B2B segment dominates e-commerce in terms of the dollar value of transactions made, B2C remains important for its potential impacts on urban travel and land use patterns.

要点概述

有迹象表明，在某种程度上，电子商务以某种形式存在于许多环境中，它明显优于传统的经商方式。因此，对于城市规划者来说，电子商务对交通运输的影响是一个相关的问题。虽然B2B部门在电子商务中占主导地位，但B2C对城市旅游和土地利用模式的潜在影响仍然很重要。

In recent years, the global B2C e-commerce market has grown rapidly, and will maintain an average annual growth rate of nearly 15% in the next few years. The transaction scale will increase from 1.6 trillion US dollars in 2014 to 3.4 trillion US dollars in 2020. Among them, global cross-border B2C e-commerce growth is particularly strong: an average annual growth of 27% will increase the global market size from $230 billion in 2014 to nearly $1 trillion in 2020. In addition, the total number of cross-border B2C e-commerce consumers will increase from 309 million in 2014 to more than 900 million in 2020, an average annual increase of more than 21%, forming a strong consumer base. Among them, the Asia-Pacific region with China as the core ranked first with 53.6% of new transaction volume contribution.

要点概述

近年来，全球B2C电商市场增长迅速，未来几年仍将保持近15%的年均增速，交易规模则将从2014年的1.6万亿美元增至2020年的3.4万亿美元。其中，全球跨境B2C电商的增长尤为强劲：年均增长高达27%的将使全球市场规模由2014年的2300亿美元升至2020年的接近1万亿美元。此外，跨境B2C电商消费者总数将由2014年的3.09亿人增加到2020年的超过9亿人，年均增幅超过21%，形成一群强劲的消费大军。其中，以中国为核心的亚太地区以53.6%的新增交易额贡献度位居首位。

4.2.2 Business to business

B2B refers to a situation where one business makes a commercial transaction with another. B2B is often contrasted with B2C. In B2B commerce, it is often the case that the parties to the relationship have comparable negotiating power, and even when they do not, each party typically involves professional staff and legal counsel in the negotiation of terms, whereas B2C is shaped to a far greater degree by economic implications of information asymmetry.We examine strategic benefits of electronic integration in B2B procurement processes as measured by gains in business from customers. The supplier derives maximum benefits when a customer initiates the system and the supplier enhances the system s capabilities. From a theoretical perspective, this scenario creates the highest reduction in transaction costs for the buyer and the maximum negative externalities for other suppliers. With respect to operational process benefits for both parties, establishing advanced EDI capabilities with customers significantly improves the performance of the order-processing system as measured by both the accuracy of order processing and timeliness of payments. Both parties benefit from reduced support resources required for the order-management function.

要点概述

B2B指的是一家公司与另一家公司进行商业交易的情况。B2B通常与B2C进行对比。在B2B商务中，通常情况下，双方的谈判能力相当，即使不是如此，双方在谈判条款时也通常都会涉及专业人员和法律顾问，而B2C在很大程度上是受信息不对称的经济影响而形成的。我们以从客户获得的业务收益衡量B2B采购过程中电子集成的战略效益。当客户启动系统并且供应商提高了系统的能力时，供应商可以获得最大的利益。从理论的角度来看，这种情况会给买家带来最高的交易成本以及其他供应商最大的负外部效应。对于双方来说，对双方的操作流程都有好处，与客户建立先进的EDI能力可以显著提高订单处理系统的性能，这是由订单处理的准确性和付款的及时性来衡量的。双方都受益于订单管理功能所需的支持资源减少。

Domestic foreign trade enterprises usually have a main business of B2B. This is because traditional foreign trade enterprises can directly transform their foreign trade mode into B2B mode based on the Internet, and the channels and rules of enterprise products and logistics are relatively perfect. B2B locates a large number of single OEMs

(OEMs) and ODMs (original design production), with a larger order amount and lower transaction batches. The way to get an order is to be publicized and sold through the Internet, and more coordination and communication with the customer is required. The relevant personnel need more patience, which makes the order consume a lot of time and energy.

要点概述

我国外贸企业通常主营业务为 B2B。这是由于传统的外贸企业能够基于互联网将自身外贸模式直接转化为 B2B 模式，企业产品、物流等渠道与规则都比较完善。B2B 定位大量单的 OEM(代工生产)和 ODM(原始设计生产)，其订单金额量比较大，交易批次也较低。得到订单的方式要通过互联网进行宣传、销售，与客户需要进行较多的协调沟通，相关人员需要较大的耐心，这使得订单需要消耗大量的时间精力。

4.2.3 Customer to customer

Customer to customer (C2C) markets provide an innovative way to allow customers to interact with each other. Traditional markets require B2C relationships, in which a customer goes to the business in order to purchase a product or service. In C2C markets, the business facilitates an environment where customers can sell goods or services to each other.

要点概述

"消费者对消费者"市场提供了一种让消费者之间可以相互交易的创新模式，传统市场需要企业对客户的交易关系，这样消费者为了购买产品或服务可以进行交易。在 C2C 这一市场中，企业促成了一种消费者之间可以互相出售产品或服务的环境。

The "consumer-to-consumer" marketing model is a process of creating products or services. Other types of markets include B2B and B2C.

要点概述

"消费者对消费者"营销模式是一种创造产品或服务的过程，其他类型的市场包括 B2B（企业对企业）、B2C（企业对消费者）。

Consumer to consumer marketing is the creation of a product or service. Other types of markets include business to business and business to customer. online C2C communication can reduce the level of uncertainty about the firm even when the individual seeking information perceives him/herself to be knowledgeable or experienced in the product. Specifically, a post-hoc content analysis11 revealed that people with higher expertise asked very specific and more technical questions about products (63% of questions asked are more specific vs. 37% of questions are broader). On the other hand, that those with lower expertise tend to ask more general/ broader questions (31% of questions asked are more specific vs. 69% of questions are broader).

要点概述

C2C是一种产品或服务的创造。其他类型的市场包括B2B和B2C。在线C2C通信可以降低企业的不确定性水平，即使是在寻求信息的个人认为自己对产品有知识或经验的情况下。具体来说，一项事后内容分析显示，拥有较高专业技能的人会就产品提出非常具体和更有技术性的问题（63%的问题更具体，37%的问题更宽泛）。另一方面，那些专业水平较低的人倾向于问更一般或更宽泛的问题（31%的问题更具体，69%的问题更宽泛）。

C2C website profit model：

(1) The membership fee；

(2) Transaction commission；

(3) Advertising；

(4) Bidding for search ranking ；

(5) Fees for the payment process。

要点概述

C2C网站盈利模式：

（1）会员费；

（2）交易提成；

（3）广告费；

（4）搜索排名竞价；

（5）支付环节收费。

4.2.4 Consumer to business

Consumer-to-business (C2B) is a business model in which consumers (individuals) create value and businesses consume that value. For example, when a consumer writes reviews or when a consumer gives a useful idea for new product development then that consumer is creating value for the business if the business adopts the input. Excepted concepts are crowd sourcing and co-creation.

要点概述

C2B是一种商业模式，在这种模式中，消费者(个人)创造价值，企业消费这种价值。例如，当消费者写评论时，或者当消费者为新产品开发提供了有用的想法时，如果企业采用了这些想法，那么消费者就是在为企业创造价值。例外的概念是众包和共同创造。

C2B model, also called a reverse auction or demand collection model, enables buyers to name or demand their own price, which is often binding, for a specific good or service. The website collects the demand bids then offers the bids to participating sellers.

要点概述

C2B模型，也被称为反向拍卖或需求收集模型，使买家能够说出或要求他们自己的价格，这通常是为特定的优质或服务提出的具有约束力的价格。该网站收集需求投标，然后向参与的卖方提供投标。

Another form of C2B is the electronic commerce business model in which consumers can offer products and services to companies, and the companies pay the consumers. This business model is a complete reversal of the traditional business model in which companies offer goods and services to consumers. We can see the C2B model at work in blogs or internet forums in which the author offers a link back to an online business thereby facilitating the purchase of a product (like a book on Amazon.com), for which the author might receive affiliate revenues from a successful sale.

要点概述

C2B的另一种形式是消费者可以向企业提供产品和服务，企业向消费者付费。这种商业模式完全颠覆了传统的商业模式，即企业向消费者提供商品和服务。我们可以在博客或互联网论坛上看到C2B模式，在这种模式下，作者提供了一个返回到在线业务的链接，从而方便购买产品(比如亚马逊网站上的一本书)，因此作者可能会从成功的销售中获得从属收入。

C2B is a consumer-to-business e-commerce website, which is different from traditional e-commerce websites. In the form of C2B e-commerce network, consumers can search for demand information without going through the C2B website. By quoting and bidding by the merchants, consumers can choose to trade with the best value-for-money merchants, so that consumers can not spend a penny, so that the merchants can sell the products without opening the store without advertising, and cut the intermediate links. More typical C2B websites have global travel, gathering and other websites.

要点概述

C2B 便是消费者对商家的电子商务网站，与传统的电子商务网站不相同，在 C2B 电子商务网的形式下消费者可以不用辛苦的去寻找商家，而是经过 C2B 网站把需求信息发布出去，由商家上来报价、竞标，消费者可以选择与性价比最佳的商家来成交，不让消费者花一分冤枉钱，让商家不开店不打广告就可以把商品卖出，削减中间环节。比较典型的 C2B 网站有全球旅拍、聚想要等网站。

Under the circumstance of rising raw material prices, the e-commerce C2B model can not only reduce the cost of SMEs, but also open up the virtual market to expand the trading quota, and make structural changes in enterprises, so that SMEs can develop into semi-virtual enterprises.

要点概述

原材料价格普遍上扬的情况下，采用电子商务C2B模式，不仅可以降低中小企业成本，而且可以打通虚拟市场扩大交易份额，进行企业结构性转变，使中小企业向半虚拟企业发展。

4.2.5 Business–Medium–Consumer

Enterprise-terminal-consumer is a new e-commerce model that uses third-party platforms to provide services including the protection of third-party quality and enterprise and consumer rights, changing network credibility crisis, and reducing enterprise operating costs. The terminal is the link and bridge between the enterprise and the consumer. It is a third-party management platform with multiple attributes such as monitoring, multimedia and broker.

要点概述

企业—终端—消费者，是一种利用第三方平台来为企业提供第三方质量、保障企业与消费者权益、改变网络诚信危机、降低企业运营成本的新型电子商务模式。终端是企业与消费者之间的纽带与桥梁，是具有监控、多媒体、经纪人等多重属性的第三方管理平台。

4.3 Comparison of the main modes of cross-border e-commerce

The current mainstream cross-border e-commerce models are mainly B2B, B2C 和 C2C the difference is mainly reflected in the participation of the main body, at the same time Show different trading characteristics. The specific differences are shown in the table below.

要点概述

目前主流的跨境电商模式主要有B2B、B2C和C2C三种，这种差异主要体现在主体的参与上，同时表现出不同的交易特征，具体差异如表4–1所示，2010—2015年我国跨境电商交易中B2B和B2C占比如图4–1所示。

表4-1 主流的跨境电商模式比较

模式	参与主体	交易特点	代表
B2B	企业与企业	大批量、小批次、集中交易	阿里巴巴国际市场、中国制造网、Directindustry
B2C	企业与消费者	小批量、多批次、碎片化	亚马逊、兰亭集势、全球速卖通
C2C	消费者与消费者	小额交易	eBay

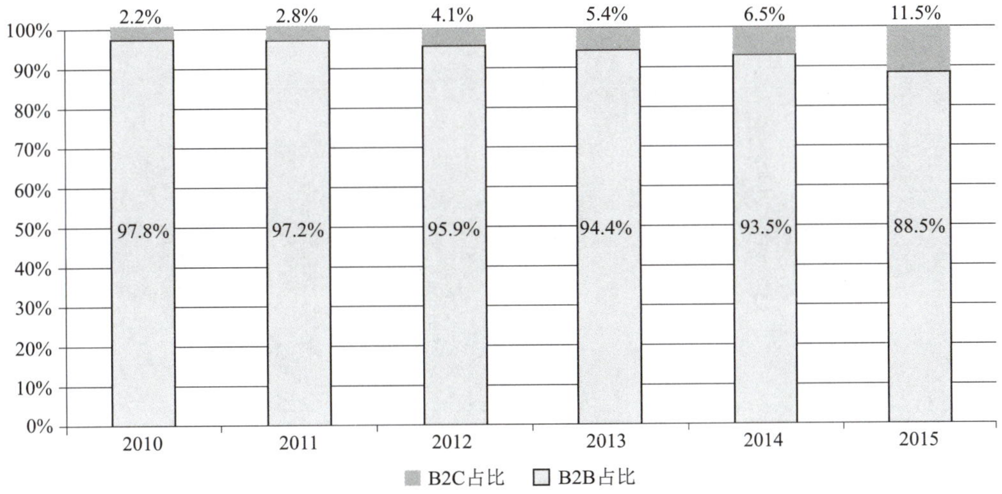

图4–1 2010—2015年中国跨境电商交易中B2B与B2C占比

Notes:

1. OEM

OEM生产，也称为定点生产，俗称代工（生产），基本含义为品牌生产者不直接生产产品，而是利用自己掌握的关键的核心技术负责设计和开发新产品，控制销售渠道。原始设备制造商具体的加工任务通过合同订购的方式委托同类产品的其他厂家生产，之后将所订产品低价买断，并直接贴上自己的品牌商标。这种委托他人生产的合作方式简称OEM，承接加工任务的制造商被称为OEM厂商，其生产的产品被称为OEM产品。可见，定点生产属于加工贸易中的“代工生产”方式，在国际贸易中是以商品为载体的劳务出口。

2. ODM

ODM（Original Design Manufacturer），直译是“原始设计制造商”。ODM是指某制造商设计出某产品后，在某些情况下可能会被另外一些企业看中，要求配上后者的品牌名称来进行生产，或者稍微修改一下设计来生产。其中，承接设计制造业务的制造商被称为ODM厂商，其生产出来的产品就是ODM产品。

Review questions:

According to the topic of this chapter, briefly answer the question:

(1) What are the main classifications of cross-border e-commerce models?

(2)What are the main drawbacks of the B2C model?

(3) The main impact of cross-border e-commerce dealers on China's import and export trade?

Chapter 5
Platform of Cross-border E-commerce

5.1 Concept of cross-border e-commerce

Cross-border e-commerce platform, which is a virtual place for exchanging information, concluding a transaction and completing Cross-border payment and settlement, is an electronic, global, open, low-cost and so on, which belongs to different national boundaries or regions, and has greatly improved the transaction efficiency of cross-border trade, It makes it possible for small and medium-sized foreign trade enterprises to have the same information resources and competitive advantages as large enterprises. Cross-border e-business is a cross-border trade based on the Internet, under the restriction of network virtuality and transaction subject virtualization, the behavior mode and value standard of the cross border transaction subject are different from the traditional transaction mode, which involves more transaction subjects, longer industrial chain, complex transaction links, and the related tax laws and policies are not unified, Through Cross-border E-commerce trading platform transactions, in the Logistics and transportation, customs inspection, tax refund and other aspects of the settlement can be better services, but also the current foreign trade enterprises and individuals to carry out cross-border trade is the main way.

要点概述

跨境电子商务平台是跨境电子化、全球化、开放化、低成本的跨境电子商务平台，属于不同的国界或地区，是信息交换、交易和完成跨境支付结算的虚拟场所，并取得了长足的进步。跨境贸易的交易效率，使得中小外贸企业能够拥有与大型企业相同的信息资源和竞争优势。跨境电子商务是基于 Internet 的跨境交易，在网络虚拟和交易主体虚拟化的限制下，跨境交易主体的行为模式和价值标准不同于传统的交易模式，其主要表现在：交易主体较多，产业链较长，交易环节复杂，相关税收法律政策不统一，通过跨境电子商务交易平台交易，在物流运输、海关检查、退税等方面结算，也是当前外贸企业和个人开展跨境贸易的主要方式。

The status of domestic cross-border e-commerce platform development. Due to the overall development trend of the domestic e-commerce industry, the cross-border e-commerce trading platform has also become a hot spot for investment by domestic and foreign venture capitalists. Since 2008, cross-border e-commerce platforms such as LightInTheBox, Treasure Island, Dalong.com, Alibaba.com, Dunhuang.com and Global Market have been favored by domestic and foreign investment institutions, with a total investment of nearly 4 billion US dollars.

▶ 要点概述

中国跨境电子商务平台发展现状。由于中国电子商务行业整体发展态势良好，跨境电子商务贸易平台也成为国内外风险投资商的投资热点。从 2008 年开始，兰亭集势、金银岛、大龙网、阿里巴巴、敦煌网、环球市场等跨境电子商务平台相继获得国内外投资机构的青睐，共获得近 40 亿美元的投资。

In the prospect of cross-border e-commerce trade in China, in addition to the domestic foreign trade e-commerce platform, the National Development and Reform Commission and the General Administration of Customs have established seven cities for piloting cross-border e-commerce services in China—Ningbo, Shanghai, Chongqing, Hangzhou, Zhengzhou, Suzhou and Shenzhen, all establishing their own cross-border e-commerce platforms based on regional advantages and their own characteristics.

▶ 要点概述

在中国跨境电子商务贸易向好的前景下，除了中国已有外贸电子商务平台外，国家发改委和海关总署确立的国家跨境贸易电子商务服务试点的 7 个城市——宁波、上海、重庆、杭州、郑州、苏州和深圳，也都纷纷结合地区优势和自身特色，建立了各自的跨境电子商务平台。

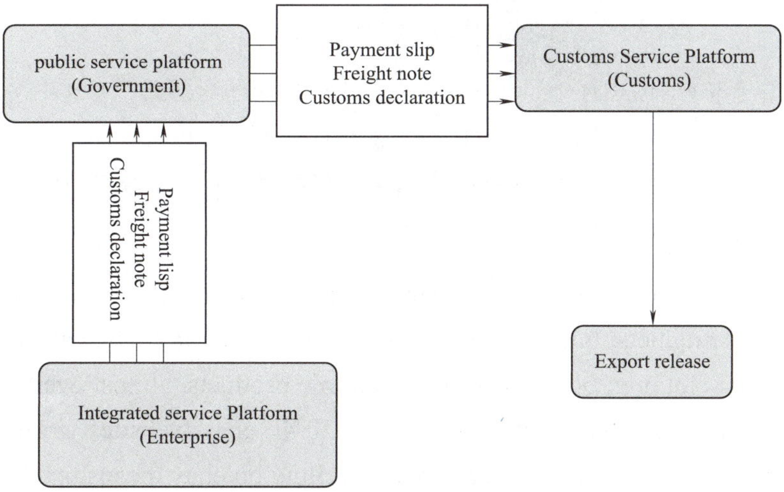

Figure 5–1 Cross-border e-commerce service diagram

5.2 Trading platform

5.2.1 eBay

EBay is a multinational e-commerce corporation, facilitating online consumer-to-consumer and business-to-consumer sales. It is headquartered in San Jose, California. EBay was founded by Pierre Omidyar in 1995, and became a notable success story of the dot-com bubble. Today eBay is a multibillion-dollar business with operations in about 30 countries.

要点概述

eBay（易贝）是一个跨国的电子商务公司，它促进互联网上“消费者对消费者”和“商家对消费者”的销售，总部设在加利福尼亚州的圣何塞。eBay 由奥米迪亚于 1995 年创立，成为互联网泡沫中一个引人注目的成功故事。如今，eBay 是一个业务遍及约 30 个国家的公司，企业价值数十亿美元。

The company manages eBay.com, an online auction and shopping website in which people and businesses buy and sell a broad variety of goods and services worldwide. In addition to its auction-style sales, the website has since expanded to include “Buy It Now” shopping; online event ticket trading and other services. It previously offered online money transfers (via PayPal, which was a wholly owned subsidiary of eBay).

要点概述

该公司负责管理 eBay 网站，它是一个在线拍卖和购物的网站。在这个网站上，人们和企业在全球范围内买卖各种商品和服务，除了拍卖式风格的销售外，该网站已经扩展到提供包括“马上购买”的购物服务、在线活动门票交易和其他服务。此前，该网站提供在线转账业务（通过 eBay 的全资子公司 PayPal 进行）。

EBay.com (ebay.com) is the nation's largest online commodity trading platform. There are not only new products, but also second-hand goods on eBay. The categories involved include used cars, clothing, books, CDs or electronic products, almost everything. eBay is an international trading platform with more than 30-40 ebay websites worldwide. PayPal can accept more than 20 mainstream currencies. Selling on ebay means that buyers all over the world will become potential users. In addition, eBay is charged, which also ensures that the business on eBay is more efficient. PayPal is generally used to pay. Most of the goods can be shipped directly to China, and transshipment is also supported. There is no US consumption tax and the rebate is lower, generally rebates 2%, Mr-rebates 3%.

要点概述

eBay 公司（ebay.com）是全美最大的在线商品交易平台。eBay 上不仅有新品，也有二手货，所涉及的类目包括二手车、服饰、书籍、CD 或电子产品等，几乎一应俱全。eBay 是国际性的买卖平台，全球有超过 30～40 个 eBay 网站。PayPal 可以接受超过 20 种主流货币，在 eBay 卖东西，意味着全球的买家都会成为潜在用户。此外 eBay 是收费的，这点也保证了在 eBay 上的生意更具有效率。在 eBay 上人们一般都用 PayPal 支付；大多数货物可直运中国，也支持转运；无美国消费税、返利较低。

5.2.2 Haitao.com

Haitao.com, or overseas shopping, is to retrieve overseas merchandise information through the Internet and send out shopping requests via an electronic order form.

要点概述

海淘网，或海外购物，是通过互联网检索海外商品信息，并通过电子订单发送购物请求。

Use of online credit cards, PayPal, etc. to complete payment payment. After receiving the order and payment information, the overseas shopping website uses the International Express mail, the postal parcel, or the forwarding company to return the goods. Consumers can freely buy goods according to their own needs and preferences.

要点概述

海外购物使用网上信用卡、PayPal 等来完成支付。海外购物网站收到订单和付款信息后，通过国际快递邮件、邮包或货运公司配送商品。消费者可以根据自己的需要和喜好自由购买商品。

On April 8, 2016, according to the Notice on the *Taxation Policy for Cross-border E-commerce Retail Imports* issued by the Ministry of Finance, the General Administration of Customs and the State Administration of Taxation, the single transaction limit for cross-border e-commerce retail imports is RMB 2,000. The annual annual trading limit is RMB 20,000. For cross-border e-commerce retail imports imported within the limits, the tariff rate is temporarily set at 0%; the value-added tax on import links and the exemption from consumption tax are temporarily levied at 70% of the statutory tax payable. A single transaction that exceeds the single limit, accumulates more than the individual annual limit, and a single indivisible commodity with a duty-paid price exceeding the limit of 2,000 yuan, is fully taxed in accordance with the general trade method. This means that if a single transaction exceeds 2,000 yuan and the individual's annual total exceeds 20,000 yuan, it will be fully taxed according to the general trade method.

要点概述

2016 年 4 月 8 日根据财政部、海关总署、国家税务总局发布的《关于跨境电子商务零售进口税收政策的通知》，跨境电子商务零售进口商品的单次交易限值为人民币 2 000 元，个人年度交易限值为人民币 20 000 元。在限值以内进口的跨境电子商务零售进口商品，关税税率暂设为 0%；进口环节增值税、消费税取消免征税额，暂按法定应纳税额的 70% 征收。超过单次限值、累加后超过个人年度限值的单次交易，以及完税价格超过 2 000 元限值的单个不可分割商品，均按照一般贸易方式全额征税。这意味着，如果单次交易超过 2 000 元、个人年度累计超过 2 万元，将按一般贸易方式全额征税。

5.2.3 Amazon

Amazon is the largest Internet e-commerce company in the United States, located in Washington State, Seattle. It is one of the first companies on the internet to start operating e-commerce. Amazon was founded in 1995 and listed on Nasdaq on May 15, 1997. Amazon, which used to run only online book sales, now has a wide range of other products that have become the world's largest online retailer and the world's second-largest internet company.

要点概述

亚马逊公司是美国最大的一家网络电子商务公司，位于华盛顿州的西雅图。它是网络上最早开始经营电子商务的公司之一。亚马逊成立于1995年，并于1997年5月15日在纳斯达克挂牌上市。一开始只经营网络的书籍销售业务，现在则扩及了范围相当广的其他产品，已成为全球商品品种最多的网上零售商和全球第二大互联网企业。

Amazon, the *Fortune* 500 company, is the largest Internet e-commerce company in the United States and has become the world's most widely used online retailer of goods. It is committed to becoming the world's most customer-centric company. Its market share and sales are very high. But the profits have been relatively low.

要点概述

亚马逊作为《财富》500强公司，是美国最大的一家网络电子商务公司，已成为全球商品种类最多的网上零售商，并致力于成为全球最以客户为中心的公司，其市场占有率和销售额都很高，但盈利一直相对较低。

- Amazon (company), an online retailer.
- Amazon Locker, Amazon. com's self-service parcel-delivery service.
- Amazon Marketplace, Amazon. com's fixed-price online marketplace.
- Amazon Web Services, Amazon. com's cloud-computing platform.
- Amazon Fresh, Amazon. com's fresh grocery platform.

要点概述

亚马逊（公司），一个在线零售商。

亚马逊储物柜，亚马逊的自助式包裹递送服务。

亚马逊市场，亚马逊的固定价格网络市场。

亚马逊网络服务，亚马逊的云计算平台。

亚马逊生鲜，亚马逊的新鲜食品杂货平台。

5.3 Payment platform

5.3.1 Electronic payment

The term electronic payment refers to a payment made from one bank account to another using electronic methods and forgoing the direct intervention of bank employees. Narrowly defined electronic payment refers to e-commerce:a payment for buying and selling goods or services offered through the Internet, or broadly to any type of electronic funds transfer.

要点概述

“电子支付”这一术语是指使用一家银行账户向另一家银行账户支付款项，交易手段是通过电子方式，并放弃银行职员的直接干预。狭义的电子支付是指电子商务——通过互联网提供的商品或服务进行买卖支付；广义上的定义是任何类型的电子资金转账。

With the development of network technology, e-commerce accelerates its development process. As a new economic fashion has been accepted by the public, online shopping groups are growing. As an important link of e-commerce, online payment has penetrated into many corners of life, and the electronic payment mode has overcome the complicated and low security characteristics of traditional payment method, which shows an important role in e-commerce. E-commerce payment method is also continuously refined and refined to meet the changing development of the industry trends and the needs of users.

要点概述

随着网络技术的不断发展，电子商务也加快了发展进程，作为新的经济时尚为大众所接受，网上购物群体不断增长。网上支付作为电子商务的重要环节也已经渗透到生活的许多角落，应运而生的电子支付方式克服了传统支付方式过程复杂、安全性低等特点，在电子商务中显现出重要作用。电子商务支付方式也在不断地细化和完善，以适应日益变化发展的行业趋势和用户需求。

5.3.2 PayPal

Established in 1998, PayPal had its initial public offering in 2002, and became a wholly owned subsidiary of eBay later that year. PayPal Holdings, Inc. is an American company operating a worldwide online payments system that supports online money transfers and serves as an electronic alternative to traditional paper methods like checks and money orders.

要点概述

成立于 1998 年的 PayPal（贝宝）在 2002 年进行首次公开发行，并于同年晚些时期成为 eBay 的全资子公司。PayPal 是一家主要经营全球性在线支付系统的美国公司，系统支持在线汇款，将其作为支票和汇票等传统纸币方式的电子替代品。

PayPal is one of the world’s largest Internet payment companies. The company operates as a payment processor for online vendors, auction sites and other commercial users, for which it charges a fee. PayPal is an account type that is designed for users with international payment requirements. It is currently the world's most widely used online trading tool. It can help us to carry out the convenient foreign trade collection, to track withdrawing and transaction, and to engage in safe international procurement and consumption.

要点概述

PayPal 是全球最大的互联网支付公司之一，该公司作为在线供应商，拍卖网站和其他商业用户的付款处理器来收取费用。PayPal 是针对具有国际收付款需求用户设计的账户类型。它是目前全球使用最为广泛的网上交易工具。它能帮助我们进行便捷的外贸收款、提现、跟踪交易、进行安全的国际采购与消费。

5.3.3 Alipay

Alipay, or Zhifubao is a third-party mobile and online payment platform in China. It was established in Hangzhou in February 2004 and was founded by Jack Ma of China's Alibaba Group. Alipay mainly provides payment and financial services. Including online purchase secured transactions, online payments, transfer, credit card repayment, mobile phone recharge, water and electricity coal payment, personal wealth management and other fields.

要点概述

阿里付，即支付宝在中国是一个第三方移动和在线支付平台，2004 年 2 月在杭州成立，创始人为中国阿里巴巴集团的马云。支付宝主要提供支付及理财服务，涉及网购担保交易、网络支付、转账、信用卡还款、手机充值、水电煤缴费、个人理财等多个领域。

Alibaba.com's Alipay is one of the most comprehensive and secure online payment system. The payment system provides buyers and sellers in two Alibaba online markets, namely Alibaba China (B2B) and Taobao.com (C2C). It solves the problem of trust in online transactions through a comprehensive payment solution while providing an effective online trading platform. Alipay customers now have three secure options: Visa cards, wire transfers and online transfers from their existing bank accounts. Alibaba will also provide Alipay to independent merchants to further expand their market opportunities, increase customer acquisition, and most importantly provide convenience to their members and customers.

要点概述

Alibaba.com 的支付宝现在是最全面、安全的在线支付系统之一，支付系统提供给买家和卖家两个阿里巴巴在线市场，分别是阿里巴巴中国 (B2B) 和 Taobao.com(C2C)，它通过一个综合的支付解决方案来解决对在线交易的信任问题，同时提供一个有效的在线交易平台。支付宝客户现在有三种安全的选择 :Visa 卡、电汇和从他们现有的银行账户在线转账。阿里巴巴还将向独立商户提供支付宝，进一步扩大其市场，增加客户获取，最重要的是为其成员和客户提供方便。

5.4 Self-built cross-border e-commerce platform model

5.4.1 Concept

With the steady development of third-party platforms, the competition among platform sellers is becoming increasingly fierce. Some powerful foreign trade companies have established their own independent cross-border B2C foreign trade e-commerce platform website. Companies such as Lightinthe-box, Milanoo, Deale Xtreme, Chinavasion, and Dinodirect are independent suppliers of domestic foreign trade companies as suppliers. The platform directly purchases goods from foreign trade enterprises, buys out the source of goods, and then builds the B2C platform to sell the goods overseas. The B2C platform provides services such as logistics, payment, and customer service. One end connects to the domestic manufacturing plant, and the other end connects overseas consumers to earn profits by earning the difference in the price of goods. The e-commerce platform enterprise itself is an independent seller, and its profit model is profit. Enterprises of this type of e-commerce model carry out the unified production or procurement, product display, online transaction of the products they operate, and deliver the products to the final consumer group through logistics and distribution. It has the characteristics of strong brand, controllable product quality and complete management system of rights trading process.

要点概述

随着第三方平台稳步发展，平台卖家之间的竞争也日渐激烈。一些实力强大的外贸企业建立起各自独立的跨境 B2C 外贸电商平台网站。如兰亭集势 (Lightinthe-box) 、米兰网 (Milanoo) 、帝科思 (Deale Xtreme) 、兴隆兴 (Chinavasion) 、大龙网 (Dinodirect) 等等。这类企业独立联系国内外贸企业作为供货商，即平台直接从外贸企业采购商品，买断货源，然后自建 B2C 平台将商品销往境外。B2C 平台提供物流、支付以及客服等服务，一端连接国内制造工厂，另一端连接境外消费者，通过赚取商品进销差价实现赢利。电商平台企业本身是独立的销售商。此类电商模式企业以标准化要求，对其经营的产品进行统一生产或者采购、产品展示、在线交易，并通过物流配送将产品投放到最终消费群体。这类企业具有品牌力强、产品质量可控以及权交易流程管理体系完备等特征。

The high level of foreign trade in the bulk manufacturing industry has created a foreign trade platform for companies to sell their products overseas. Most of the above Cross-border electricity dealers through the formation of their own set of channel supply chain, sales of specific types of products. There are two notable features: product concentration differentiation and small packaging of goods. The so-called product concentration differentiation means that most of these electric dealers choose one or more kinds of products with higher profit, such as 3C digital, wedding and so on, and the small packaging of goods refers to their customers are mostly terminal consumers, no need for bulk goods logistics, but only a specific international express to solve. The value chain of the self-built cross-border electric business platform model is the same as that of the traditional enterprise, including the basic activities and the supporting activities. The core value creation process of the self-built cross-border electric power supplier lies in the control and marketing of its production cost. It is an important way to improve the profit of the electric power suppliers to use the micro-cross-border electronic commerce method to sell the products to the international market with higher profit margin.

要点概述

大宗制造业的外贸门槛较高，所以催生了企业自建外贸平台来向海外销售自己的产品。上述几个跨境电商大都通过组建自己一整套的渠道供应链，销售特定类型的产品。它们有两个显著的特点：产品集中差异化以及货物的小包化。所谓产品集中差异化是指这类电商大都选取一类或几种利润比较高的产品，如3C数码、婚纱等；而货物的小包化则指的是他们的客户大多是终端的消费者，无须大宗货物的物流，而只需要特定的国际快递来解决。自建跨境电商平台模式的价值链与传统企业的价值链一样，也包括基础活动与支持性活动。自建跨境供电企业的核心价值创造过程在于对其生产成本的控制和营销。利用微跨境电子商务方法将产品以更高的利润率销售到国际市场，是提高供电企业利润的重要途径。

5.4.2 Advantages

1) Design Freedom

Self-built cross-border e-commerce platform can be designed according to product characteristics and style, achieve personalized features, highlight product features, get rid of many rules and restrictions of third-party platforms, abandon the shortcomings of the single store model, better reflect the strength of the enterprise and win the trust of buyers.

要点概述

1）设计自由

自建跨境电商平台可以根据产品特点和风格进行设计，可以实现个性化特点，突出产品特色，摆脱第三方平台的很多规则限制，摒弃网店模式单一的缺点，更好地体现企业的实力及赢得买家的信任。

2) Easy to promote

Self-built Cross-border e-commerce platform has a separate domain name, independent IP, unique style and name. It is easier for it to use search engines, social media marketing, and other ways to promote, and traffic directly to the respective website, the probability of the closure of customers significantly reduced.

要点概述

2）易于推广

自建跨境电商平台拥有独立域名、独立 IP、独特的风格与名称，更容易利用搜索引擎、社会化媒体营销等方式进行推广，并且流量直接指向各自网站，客户被截流的概率大幅降低。

3) Feature-rich

Self-built multinational e-commerce platform has powerful functions, such as notifying friends, vouchers, account management, product evaluation, promotion, site map and other functions, solving many problems for foreign trade partners, and vigorously promoting the development of foreign trade business.

要点概述

3）功能强大

自建跨国电子商务平台具有强大的功能，如通知朋友、凭证、账务管理、产品评估、促销、站点地图等，为外贸合作伙伴解决了许多难题，大力促进了外贸业务的发展。

4) Cost savings

Since the introduction of the third-party platform model, it has undergone a period of transformation and transformation. From the initial free third-party foreign trade platform to the increasingly fierce competition of platform sellers, the advertising fees and promotion fees of sellers are increasing. In comparison, self-built cross-border e-commerce platforms can effectively save costs. At present, many foreign trade e-commerce companies choose to continue to use the third-party platform, while building independent self-owned foreign trade websites, using third-party platforms to tap customer resources, and then attract customers to their foreign trade websites, which is conducive to cost savings and to the brand building of enterprises.

要点概述

4）节约成本

第三方平台模式自面世至今，历经阶段性转型演变，由最初的免费第三方外贸平台，到平台卖家竞争日益激烈，卖家的广告费、推广费日益增加。相比较而言，自建跨境电商平台能够有效节约成本。目前，很多外贸电商企业选择继续借势第三方平台，同时建设独立的自有外贸网站，利用第三方平台挖掘客户资源，然后把客户吸引到自己的外贸网站，这样既有利于节约成本，还有利于企业的品牌建设。

Note

1. VISA

VISA 卡是维萨国际组织从 1982 年末开始发行的，其前身美洲银行。成立于 1959 年，在美国加利福尼亚州发行美洲银行卡 (Bank-Americard)。1977 年更名为 Visa，并发行第一张借记卡，1987 年推出多币种清算结算服务。

2. 电汇

电汇是付款人将一定款项交存汇款银行，汇款银行通过电报或电传传给目的地的分行或代理行（汇入行），指示汇入行向收款人支付一定金额的一种交款方式。

3. 兰亭集势

兰亭集势（Lightinthe-box）是中国整合了供应链服务的在线 B2C，该公司拥有一系列的供应商，并拥有自己的数据仓库和长期的物流合作伙伴，截止到 2010 年兰亭集势是中国跨境电子商务平台的领头羊。

4. 米兰网

米兰网是外贸电子商务企业，公司在北京等地分别建有运营中心、供应商招商中心、全球物流配送中心，有 3000 多平方米的办公场地和上万平方米的物流仓储中心。

Review questions:

According to the topic of this chapter, briefly answer the following questions:

(1) List some types of trading platform ?

(2) List some types of payment platform ?

(3) Briefly introduce some information you know about Alipay ?

(4) Talk about the advantages of Self-built Cross-border e-commerce platform.

Chapter 6

International Logistics Services Pattern

6.1 Concept of cross-border logistics

In the process of Cross-border e-commerce operation, the information flow, business flow and capital flow can be realized under the virtual environment, but the logistics link can't. Cross-border logistics refers to logistics service between two or more countries, which is a form of logistics service development to advanced stage. Because cross-border e-commerce transactions are divided into different countries, the commodity needs to be transferred from the supplier country through cross-border logistics to achieve the final logistics and distribution in the country where the demand side is located.

要点概述

在跨境电子商务运作过程中，信息流、商流和资金流均可在虚拟环境下实现，但物流环节是不能在虚拟环境下实现的。跨境物流指在两个或两个以上国家之间进行的物流服务，是物流服务发展到高级阶段的一种表现形式。由于跨境电子商务的交易双方分属不同国家，商品需要从供应方国家通过跨境物流方式实现空间位置转移，在需求方所在国家内实现最后的物流与配送。

6.2 Classification of cross-border Logistics

Cross-border logistics can be divided into nine types as a whole: ①International Postal Parcel; ② International Express; ③ International Logistics Line; ④ Overseas

Warehouse; ⑤ Frontier Warehouse; ⑥ Bonded area, free trade Zone logistics; ⑦ Set Cargo flow; ⑧ Third party Logistics; ⑨ Fourth Party Logistics.

要点概述

跨境物流总体上可分为九类：①国际邮包；②国际快递；③国际物流线；④海外仓库；⑤边境仓库；⑥保税区、自由贸易区物流；⑦固定货物流；⑧第三方物流；⑨第四方物流。

6.2.1 Third-party logistics

Third-party logistics (abbreviated 3PL, or sometimes TPL) in logistics and supply chain management is a company's use of third-party businesses to outsource elements of the company's distribution and fulfillment services.

要点概述

在物流和供应链管理中，第三方物流（简称 3PL，也称 TPL）是公司利用第三方业务将公司分销和履约的要素外包。

Third-party logistics providers typically specialize in integrated operation, warehousing and transportation services which can be scaled and customized to customers' needs based on market conditions, such as the demands and delivery service requirements for their products and materials. Often, these services go beyond logistics and include value-added services related to the production or procurement of goods, i.e., services that integrate parts of the supply chain. When this integration occurs, the provider is then called a third-party supply chain management provider (3PSCM) or supply chain management service provider (SCMSP). 3PL targets particular functions within supply management, such as warehousing, transportation, or raw material provision.

要点概述

第三方物流提供商通常专门从事综合经营、仓储和运输服务，这些服务可根据市场条件，如产品和材料的需求和交货服务要求，根据客户的需求进行规模化和定制。通常，这些服务超出了物流的范围，包括与商品的生产或采购有关的增值服务，即集成供应链各部分的服务。当这种集成发生时，提供者被称为第三方供应链管理提供者（3PSCM）或供应链管理服务提供者（SCMSP）。3PL 针对供应管理中的特定职能，如仓储、运输或原材料供应。

With the development of information technology and the trend of economic globalization, more and more products are circulating, producing, selling and consuming in the world. The logistics activities are increasingly large and complex, and the organization and operation methods of the first and second parties have been unable to satisfy the needs of the society. At the same time, in order to participate in the world competition, enterprises must establish core competitiveness, strengthen supply chain management, reduce logistics costs, and outsource logistics activities that are not core businesses. As a result, third-party logistics came into being.

要点概述

随着信息技术的发展和经济全球化趋势，越来越多的产品在世界范围内流通、生产、销售和消费，物流活动日益庞大和复杂，而第一、二方物流的组织和经营方式已不能完全满足社会需要；同时，为参与世界性竞争，企业必须确立核心竞争力，加强供应链管理，降低物流成本，把不属于核心业务的物流活动外包出去。于是，第三方物流应运而生。

Third-party logistics involves the use of external companies to perform logistics functions that are traditionally performed within the organization. Functions performed by third parties may cover the entire logistics process or selected activities in the process [2].

要点概述

第三方物流涉及使用外部公司来执行传统上在组织内执行的物流功能。第三方履行的职能可以涵盖整个物流过程或在该过程中所选择的活动。

In 2014, the global 3PL market reached US$750 billion, and the US grew to US$157 billion. The US 3PL service demand growth (7.4%) exceeded the US economic growth in 2014. As of 2014, among *Fortune* 500 companies, 80% of companies and 96 of the *Fortune* 100 companies used some form of 3PL services. It is estimated that from 2016 to 2024, the global third-party logistics market will grow by about 5%. The company manages logistics enterprises (prediction, warehousing, transportation management software) for the shipping industry. By 2024, the market will reach $10.54 billion.

要点概述

2014 年全球 3PL 市场达到 7 500 亿美元，美国增长到 1 570 亿美元；美国 3PL 服务需求增长 (7.4%) 超过了 2014 年美国经济的增长。截至 2014 年，在《财富》500 强公司中，80% 的公司和《财富》100 强中有 96 家采用了某种形式的 3PL 服务。预计 2024 年前全球第三方物流市场将增长 5% 左右，市场的规模将达到 105.4 亿美元。

2 Skjoett-Larsen T. Third party logistics: from an interorganizational point of view[J]. International Journal of Physical Distribution & Logistics Management, 2000, 30(2):112-127.

Within the last few years, however, there has been a pronounced change in shipper-logistics provider arrangements. While the primary driving forces previously were to reduce costs and release capital to alternative purposes, the driving forces today have a more strategic trust: to increase market coverage, improve the level of service or increase flexibility towards the changing requirements of customers. Cooperation between the parties has become more long-term in nature, mutually binding and is often combined with changes in both organization and information systems. Solutions are tailored to specific services and often include value-adding services such as final assembly, packaging, quality control, and information services, to name a few. This broader, more flexible cooperative arrangement is termed third party logistics (TPL). It is also known under other names as logistics alliances.[2]

要点概述

然而，在过去的几年里，托运人—物流供应商的安排有了明显的变化。虽然以前的主要驱动力是降低成本和将资金用于其他目的，但今天的驱动力具有更加战略性的信任：增加市场覆盖面、提高服务水平或增加对客户不断变化的需求的灵活性。双方之间的合作在本质上已经变得更加长期、相互约束并且经常与组织和信息系统的变化相结合。解决方案是专门针对特定服务的，并且通常包括增值服务，例如，最终组装、包装、质量控制和信息服务。这种更广泛、更灵活的合作安排被称为第三方物流（TPL）。它也有物流联盟等其他名称。

The HAVI Group, founded in 1974 in Chicago, USA, to meet the needs of McDonald's. It is a logistics company with the world's leading multi-temperature food distribution technology. With a global presence, it provides quality distribution services to McDonald's restaurants around the world and is an important member of the McDonald's food supply chain. HAVI is more than just a transportation company. It also provides value-added services such as food light processing for McDonald's.

要点概述

美国夏晖集团 (HAVI Group)，1974 年为满足麦当劳的需求创立于美国芝加哥。它是一家拥有世界领先的多温度食品分发技术的物流公司，业务遍及全球，为麦当劳全球几千余家餐厅提供优质的分发服务，是麦当劳食品供应链的重要成员之一。夏晖不仅仅是一个运输公司，它还为麦当劳提供食品轻加工等增值服务。

6.2.2 Fourth party logistics

The fourth party logistics refers to the designed for both parties, the third party logistics planning, consulting, logistics information system, supply chain management, and other services, through the deployment and management and complementary resources, capabilities, and technology service providers, to provide comprehensive, integrated supply chain solutions. The fourth party logistics, through the influence of the whole supply chain, integrates various social resources to realize the full utilization of logistics information sharing and social logistics resources on the basis of solving the enterprise logistics. Based on the complexity of cross-border e-commerce and cross-border logistics, a number of fourth party logistics enterprises have emerged to inject new factors into cross-border logistics. On January 26, 2015, announced the official launch of lanting collection of potential " Lanting z-tone" global cross-border logistics open platform, to integrate logistics service resources across the globe, providing open bid price comparison, global intelligent path optimization, multiple cooperating logistic distribution, automatic single documentary, big data intelligent analysis and other services.

要点概述

第四方物流指专为交易双方和第三方提供物流规划、咨询、物流信息系统、供应链管理等服务，通过调配与管理自身及具有互补性的服务提供商的资源、能力和技术，提供综合、全面的供应链解决方案。第四方物流通过整个供应链的影响力，在解决企业物流的基础上，整合各类社会资源，实现物流信息共享与社会物流资源充分利用。基于跨境电子商务与跨境物流的复杂性，涌现出一批第四方物流模式企业，为跨境物流注入新鲜因素。如2015年1月26日，兰亭集势宣布正式启动“兰亭智通”全球跨境物流开放平台，以整合全球各地物流配送服务资源，提供开放的比价竞价、全球智能路径优化、多物流商协同配送、自动打单跟单、大数据智能分析等服务。

6.2.3 Overseas warehousing

A warehouse is a commercial building for storage of goods. Warehouses are used by manufacturers, importers, exporters, wholesalers, transport businesses, customs, etc. They are usually large plain buildings in industrial areas of cities, towns and villages. As in warehousing, there are different types of cross docks. Reverse logistics is another type of warehousing that has become popular.

They usually have loading docks to load and unload goods from trucks. Sometimes warehouses are designed for the loading and unloading of goods directly from railways, airports, or seaports. They often have cranes and forklifts for moving goods, which are usually placed on ISO standard pallets loaded into pallet racks. Stored goods can include any raw materials, packing materials, spare parts, components, or finished goods associated with agriculture, manufacturing and production. In Indian a warehouse may be referred to as a go down.

要点概述

仓库是用来储存货物的商业建筑。仓库被制造商、进口商、出口商、批发商、运输业、海关等使用，它们通常是城市、城镇和村庄工业地区的大型平原建筑。在仓储方面，有不同类型的十字码头。逆向物流是另一种流行的仓储。

通常装载码头用卡车装卸货物，另一些仓库则专门为直接从铁路、机场或港口装卸货物而设计。它们通常有起重机和叉车来搬运货物，这些货物通常放在装有托盘货架上的ISO标准托盘上。储存的货物可以包括任何原材料、包装材料、备件、零部件或与农业、制造和生产相关的成品。

Traditional warehousing has declined since the last decades of the 20th century, with the gradual introduction of Just In Time (JIT) techniques. The JIT system promotes product delivery directly from suppliers to consumer without the use of warehouses. However, with the gradual implementation of offshore outsourcing and offshoring in about the same time period, the distance between the manufacturer and the retailer (or the parts manufacturer and the industrial plant) grew considerably in many domains, necessitating at least one warehouse per country or per region in any typical supply chain for a given range of products.

要点概述

现代仓库通常采用宽通道托盘系统来储存货物，可以用叉车装载和卸载。传统仓储使用率在20世纪末因技术进步而下降。JIT系统促进产品直接从供应商交付给消费者，而不再需要使用仓库。然而随着离岸外包和离岸开发的逐步实现，制造商和零售商之间的距离（或零部件制造商和工业厂房）大幅延伸。

Recent retailing trends have led to the development of warehouse-style retail stores. These high-ceiling buildings display retail goods on tall, heavy duty industrial racks rather than conventional retail shelving. Typically, items ready for sale are on the bottom of the racks, and crated or palatalized inventory is in the upper rack. Essentially, the same building serves as both warehouse and retail store.

要点概述

最近的零售趋势导致了仓储式零售商店的发展。这些高天花板的建筑展示了高、重型工业货架而不是传统零售货架上的零售商品。通常情况下，准备出售的物品在货架的底部，而板条箱或托盘化的库存在上层。同一栋楼本质上既是仓库，也是零售商店。

6.3 Main international express

6.3.1 DHL express

DHL express is a division of the German logistics company providing international courier, parcel and express mail services. Deutsche Post DHL is the world's largest logistics company operating around the world, particularly in sea and air mail. It provides an unrivalled portfolio of logistics services ranging from national and international parcel delivery, e-commerce shipping and fulfillment solutions, international express, road, air and ocean transport to industrial supply chain management. DHL is decisively positioned as "The logistics company for the world".

要点概述

敦豪快递是一家提供国际快递、包裹和快件服务的德国快递公司。德国邮政 DHL 是世界上最大的在世界各地运作的物流公司，尤其是海上和航空邮件方面。DHL 提供了无与伦比的物流服务组合，从国际国内包裹递送、电子商务运输、物流解决方案、国际快递，到公路、航空和海洋运输和工业化供应链管理。它被定位为“世界物流公司”。

Founded in the United States in 1969 to deliver documents between San Francisco and Honolulu, the company expanded its service throughout the world by the late 1970s. The company was primarily interested in offshore and inter-continental deliveries, but the success of FedEx prompted their own intra-US expansion starting in 1983.

要点概述

该公司于 1969 年在美国成立，开始是在旧金山和檀香山之间递送文件，在 20 世纪 70 年代末扩大了在世界各地的服务。该公司主要对离岸和洲际的交付感兴趣，但联邦快递的成功促使他们自 1983 年开始在美国内部扩张。

In 1998, Deutsche Post began to acquire shares in DHL. It reached majority ownership in 2001, and 100% ownership by December 2002. The company then absorbed DHL into its Express division, while expanding the use of the DHL brand to other Deutsche Post divisions, business units and subsidiaries. Today, DHL Express shares its DHL brand with business units such as DHL Global Forwarding and DHL Supply Chain.

要点概述

在 1998 年，德国邮政开始收购 DHL 的股票。该公司在 2001 年取得了多数股权，到 2002 年 12 月拥有 100% 的所有权。公司之后吸收了 DHL 进入分部，同时拓宽了对 DHL 品牌的用途，扩大到其他邮政部门、业务单位和附属部门。今天，DHL 快递与 DHL 全球货运和 DHL 供应链等业务部门共享该品牌。

The DHL Express financial results are published in the Deutsche Post AG annual report. In 2016, this division's revenue increased by 2.7 per cent to € 14 billion. The earnings before interest and taxes (EBIT) increased by 11.3% over 2015 to € 1.5 billion.

要点概述

DHL 快递的财务结果发表在德意志银行的年度报告中。2016 年，该司的收入增加了 2.7%，至 140 亿欧元。利息和税前的收益增加了 11.3%，超过了 2015 年的 15 亿欧元。

6.3.2 United Parcel Service

United Parcel Service was founded in 1907. It has locations in the United States as well as around the world. Its corporate headquarters is located in Atlanta, Georgia. UPS is the world's largest package distribution company delivering more than 13 million documents and parcels every day and generating revenues of more than $27 billion a year. UPS is also the world's largest express package and document delivery company, delivering more packages in two days or less that are tracked and guaranteed than any other company in the industry. It serves more than 200 countries and territories. The company operates in five international regions: Europe/Middle East & Africa; Asia Pacific; Latin America/Caribbean; Canada and the United States. The company is broken down into several divisions because of this. These divisions include UPS Air Cargo, UPS Aviation Technologies, UPS Capital Corporation, UPS Consulting, UPS Mail Innovations, Mail Boxes Etc., Inc., UPS Professional Services, UPS Supply Chain Solutions, and UPS Tele Services.

要点概述

联合包裹服务公司成立于 1907 年。它在美国和世界各地都有分布。公司总部位于佐治亚州的亚特兰大。UPS 是全球最大的快递公司，每天递送超过 1300 万份文件和包裹，每年的收入超过 270 亿美元。UPS 也是世界上最大的快递包裹和文件递送公司，在两天或更短的时间内交付的包裹比其他任何公司都要多。它服务于 200 多个国家和地区。该公司在欧洲、中东、非洲五个地区开展业务：亚太地区、拉丁美洲、加勒比海、加拿大和美国。由于这个原因，公司分成了几个部门。这些部门包括 UPS 航空货运公司、联合包裹航空技术公司、UPS 资本公司、UPS 咨询公司、UPS 邮件创新公司、UPS 的专业服务公司、UPS 供应链解决方案公司和 UPS 电信服务公司。

6.3.3 Express mail service

Express mail is an accelerated mail delivery service for which the customer pays a surcharge and receives faster delivery. Express mail is a service for domestic and international mail and is in most countries governed by a country's own postal administration. Since 1998, the international accelerated delivery services are governed by the EMS Cooperative.

要点概述

特快邮件是一种客户支付额外费用可以收到更快邮件的邮件传递服务。快递邮件是国内和国际邮件的服务，在大多数国家由本国邮政管理。自 1998 年以来，国际加速交付服务由 EMS 合作社管理。

6.4 The selection of cross-border logistics mode

Under the background of today's cross-border e-commerce, cross-border logistics needs to change the traditional large orders, bulk and scale of the operation management mode, conforms to the cross-border electronic business logistics characteristics such as small batch, batches, short cycle, the international logistics system in the transport, storage, management, and other links to upgrade. At the same time, cross-border e-commerce enterprises should combine their own capabilities to rationally choose cross-border logistics mode, reduce logistics costs and improve service efficiency. The following are some general patterns of cross-border logistics in China.

要点概述

在当今跨境商务的背景下，跨境物流需要改变传统的大订单、大批量、大规模的运营管理模式，转为符合跨境电子商务物流的小批量、短周期、低成本的特点，从而实现跨国物流系统在运输、仓储、管理等环节的升级换代。同时，跨境电子商务企业应结合自身能力，合理选择跨境物流模式，降低物流成本，提高服务效率。以下是中国跨境物流的一般模式。

Cross-border e-commerce logistics is still a relatively new concept in the field of logistics. International trade import and export usually involves international settlement, import and export customs clearance, international transportation, logistics insurance, etc., but also needs to consider factors such as safety and risk control. Cross-border e-commerce promotes and accelerates the process of global economic integration, making the development of the logistics industry a global intensification trend. In developed countries such as Europe and the United States, cross-border e-commerce started earlier, represented by eBay and Amazon. The efficient logistics system in developed countries provides strong support for this.

要点概述

跨境电子商务物流在物流学界还是一个比较新的概念。国际贸易进出口通常涉及国际结算、进出口通关、国际运输、物流保险等环节，同时还需要考虑其安全性及风险控制等因素。跨境电子商务推动并加速全球经济一体化进程，使物流产业发展呈现全球性集约化趋势。在欧美等发达国家，跨境电子商务起步较早，代表企业有易趣、亚马逊等。发达国家的高效物流体系为此提供了有力支撑。

6.4.1 Cross–border e–commerce export logistics mode

According to incomplete statistics, China's current cross-border e-commerce has more than 60 percent of the goods shipped through the postal system. China post actively carries out cross-border logistics and express delivery service, and has customized the new international postal and delivery products for eBay China sellers. International e post is a new economical international mail delivery product tailored for Chinese e-commerce vendors to meet the needs of the international e-commerce delivery market. International e mail treasure and the Hong Kong international as for light small items of airmail parcel service products. At present, the business is limited to provide Chinese electricity sellers sender sent to the United States, Canada, Britain, France and Australia package Posting and delivering services. The international e-mail treasure economy is economical, support to be charged according to the total weight, 50 grams first weight, continue to be calculated according to each gram, free registration fee. In 2013, the international e - mail service has covered more than 40 cities in China, with an average daily processing of 100,000 parcels. although China post has a global postal network, it still has a long transportation time and high packet loss rate in terms of logistics service level.

要点概述

据不完全统计，中国目前跨境电子商务有超过 60% 的商品通过邮政体系运输。中国邮政积极开展跨境物流快递业务，为 eBay 中国大陆卖家量身定制了全新国际邮递产品——国际 e 邮宝。国际 e 邮宝是中国邮政为适应国际电子商务寄递市场的需要，为中国电商卖家量身定制的一款全新经济型国际邮递产品。国际 e 邮宝和香港国际小包服务一样是针对轻小件物品的空邮产品，目前，该业务限于为中国电商卖家寄件人提供发向美国、加拿大、英国、法国和澳大利亚的包裹寄递服务。国际 e 邮宝经济实惠，支持按总重计费，50 克首重，续重按照每克计算，免收挂号费。2013 年，国际 e 邮宝服务已覆盖中国 40 多个城市，日均处理包裹达 10 万件。中国邮政虽然拥有覆盖全球的邮政网络，但在物流服务水平上仍存在运输时间长、丢包率高等问题。

6.4.2 Cross-border e-commerce import logistics mode

The import logistics mode under the cross-border e-commerce environment mainly includes direct mail mode and transport mode. Among them, direct mail mode is divided into commercial express direct mail and two countries express cooperation direct mail; The transport mode has sunshine overseas online shopping and grey overseas online shopping.

The specific cross-border e-commerce import logistics mode is analyzed and shown in the following figure.

要点概述

跨境电子商务环境下的进口物流模式主要包括直邮模式和运输模式。其中，直邮模式分为商业快递直邮和两国快递合作直邮；运输模式有阳光海外网购和灰色海外网购。具体的跨境电子商务进口物流模式分析如图 6–1 所示。

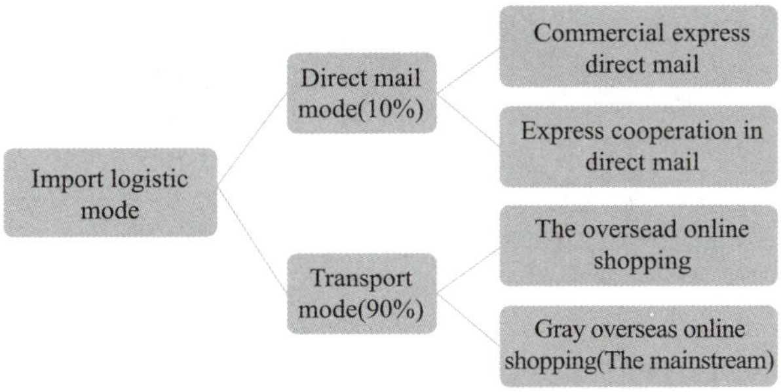

Figure 6–1 Cross-border e-commerce import logistics mode [3]

Notes:

1. 流通加工

流通加工是产品在从生产者向消费者流通过程中，为了增加附加价值，满足客户需求，

---

[3] 罗亚康．中小企业跨境电商物流渠道的选择 [J]. 商场现代化 ,2015,15:43-44.

Data source: 庞燕，跨境电商环境下国际物流模式研究．

促进销售而进行简单的组装、剪切、套裁、贴标签、刷标志、分类、检量，弯管、打孔等加工作业。

2. 逆向物流

逆向物流（reverse logistics）是指，商家客户委托第三方物流公司将交寄物品从用户指定所在地送达商家客户所在地的过程。对于企业而言，逆向物流往往出于以下动机：环境管制；经济利益（体现在废弃物处理费用的减少、产品寿命的延长、原材料零部件的节省等方面）和商业考虑。

3. 准时生产方式

准时制生产方式（Just In Time，JIT），又称作无库存生产方式（stockless production），零库存（zero inventories），一个流（one-piece flow）或者超级市场生产方式（supermarket production）。

Chapter 7

Technology of Cross-border E-commerce

7.1 Electronic data interchange

7.1.1 Definition

Electronic data interchange(EDI) is the concept of electronically communicating information traditionally conveyed on paper. Two typical examples of this type of information are purchase orders and invoices. The significance of the EDI standard is to facilitate the parties to conduct transactions without having to make special arrangements.

要点概述

电子数据交换（EDI）是企业通过电子方式来传达传统上某些用纸张传达的信息的概念。这类信息的两个典型例子是采购订单和发票。EDI 标准存在的意义是为了方便当事人进行交易，而不必制定特别的安排。

Electronic data interchange reduces the consumption of paper documents, reduces duplication of effort, increases work efficiency, and enables traders to trade in a more rapid and efficient manner. It greatly simplifies the ordering process or inventory process, enabling both parties to make full use of their human and material resources in a timely manner. It can improve the relationship between the two parties, so that manufacturers can accurately estimate the demand for goods in the future, freight forwarders can simplify a large number of export paperwork, business users can improve inventory efficiency and improve their competitiveness.

要点概述

电子数据交换降低了纸张文件的消费；减少了许多重复劳动，提高了工作效率；使得贸易双方能够以更迅速、有效的方式进行贸易，大大简化了订货过程或存货过程，使双方能及时地充分利用各自的人力和物力资源；可以改善贸易双方的关系，厂商可以准确地估计日后商品的需求量，货运代理商可以简化大量的出口文书工作，商业用户可以提高存货的效率，提高他们的竞争能力。

7.1.2 Characteristic

EDI has existed for more than 30 years, and there are many EDI standards (including X12, EDIFACT, ODETTE, etc.), some of which address the needs of specific industries or regions. It also refers specifically to a family of standards. In 1996, the National Institute of Standards and Technology defined electronic data interchange as "the computer-to-computer interchange of strictly formatted messages that represent documents other than monetary instruments. EDI implies a sequence of messages between two parties, either of whom may serve as originator or recipient. The formatted data representing the documents may be transmitted from originator to recipient via telecommunications or physically transported on electronic storage media." It distinguishes mere electronic communication or data exchange, specifying that in EDI, the usual processing of received messages is by computer only. Human intervention in the processing of a received message is typically intended only for error conditions, for quality review, and for special situations. For example, the transmission of binary or textual data is not EDI as defined here unless the data are treated as one or more data elements of an EDI message and are not normally intended for human interpretation as part of online data processing. EDI can be formally defined as the transfer of structured data, by agreed message standards, from one computer system to another without human intervention.

要点概述

EDI 已经存在了 30 多年，EDI 标准很多（包括 X12，EDIFACT，ODETTE 等），其中一些标准满足了特定行业或地区的需求。它也专指一个标准家族。1996 年，国家标准与技术研究院将电子数据交换定义为“计算机与计算机之间交换严格格式化消息，代表货币工具以外的其他文件，EDI 意味着双方之间的一系列消息，其中任何一方都可以作为发起方或接收方，格式化的数据代表文件可以通过电信从发信人传送到接收人，也可以通过电子存储媒体物理传送。”它区分纯粹的电子通信或数据交换，在 EDI 中，接收到的消息的通常处理仅由计算机进行处理。人工干预处理接收到的消息通常仅用于错误状况，用于质量评审，以及特殊情况，例如，电子数据交换可以正式定义为，通过商定的信息标准将结构化数据从一个计算机系统转移到另一个计算机系统，而无须人为干预。

The manufacturing industry uses EDI to fully understand and meet the needs of customers, formulate a supply plan to reduce inventory and accelerate capital flow. The transport industry uses EDI to realize the electronic data transmission of freight documents, making full use of transportation equipment and positions to provide high level and fast service for customers.

For the storage industry, EDI can accelerate the extraction and turnover of goods, reduce the tension of storage space contradictions, thereby increasing utilization

要点概述

制造业利用 EDI 能充分理解并满足客户的需要，制订出供应计划，达到降低库存，加快资金流动的目的。运输业采用 EDI 能实现货运单证的电子数据传输，充分利用运输设备、仓位，为客户提供高层次和快捷的服务。对仓储业，可加速货物的提取及周转，减缓仓储空间紧张的矛盾，从而提高利用率。

7.1.3 Challenges in EDI implementation[4]

Companies that have enabled EDI face many challenges related to EDI application management. The company is going through:

(1) Limited solution options.

(2) Unable to trade with the entire business community or meet regulatory compliance requirements.

(3) Low quality of service and high cost.

(4) Limited or poor customer service.

In addition, companies that wish to implement EDI procedures often find their options limited. Other challenges include:

(1) Expensive solutions, which is not a cost-effective situation.

(2) Technical requirements are beyond their capabilities.

(3) Limited support or implementation.

(4) Unable to meet with trading partners.

4 Benson Mugambi Njoni, Schola Semutwa, Morris Gitonga Mbaabu, Job Onyinkwa Osoro. Application of Electronic Data Interchange in Logistics: A Case of Nas Hauliers, Rwanda[J]. Journal of Logistics Management 2016, 5(2): 39-47

要点概述

已经启用 EDI 的公司面临着与 EDI 应用程序管理相关的许多挑战。公司正在经历：

（1）有限的解决方案选择。

（2）无法与整个业务社区进行交易或满足法规遵从性要求。

（3）服务质量低，成本高。

（4）有限或较差的客户服务。

此外，希望实施 EDI 程序的公司通常会发现他们的选择是有限的。其他挑战包括：

（1）昂贵的解决方案，这是不符合成本效益的情况。

（2）技术要求超出了他们的能力。

（3）有限的支持或实施。

（4）无法与贸易伙伴见面。

The implementation of EDI has been claimed to be vital for the success of international trade, as it requires bundle of data exchanges between many parties across geographical boundaries.

要点概述

电子数据交换的实施被认为对国际贸易的成功至关重要，因为它要求跨地理边界的许多缔约方之间进行数据交换。

7.2 Big Data

7.2.1 Definition

Big data is data sets that are so large or complex that traditional data processing application software is inadequate to deal with them. Big data challenges include capturing data, data storage, data analysis, search, sharing, transfer, visualization, querying, updating and information privacy. Big Data, also known as massive data, refers to the massive, high-growth, and diverse information assets that require new processing models to have greater decision-making, insight, and process optimization capabilities.

要点概述

大数据是如此庞大或复杂的数据集，以至于传统的数据处理应用软件不足以处理它们。大数据挑战包括捕获数据、数据存储、数据分析、搜索、共享、传输、可视化、查询、更新和信息隐私。大数据（Big Data）又称为巨量资料，指需要新处理模式才能具有更强的决策力、洞察力和流程优化能力的海量、高增长率和多样化的信息资产。

The value of large data is embodied in the following areas:

(1) Enterprises with a large number of consumers to provide products or services can use large data for precision marketing

(2) Small and beautiful micro-enterprises can use large data to do service transformation

(3) The traditional enterprises that must be transformed under the pressure of internet need to keep pace with time and make full use of the value of large data.

要点概述

大数据的价值体现在以下几个方面：

（1）对大量消费者提供产品或服务的企业可以利用大数据进行精准营销。

（2）做小而美模式的中小微企业可以利用大数据做服务转型。

（3）面临互联网压力之下必须转型的传统企业需要与时俱进，充分利用大数据的价值。

7.2.2 Characteristics

Big data can be described by the following characteristics:

要点概述

可以用以下特点描述大数据：

(1) Volume. The quantity of generated and stored data. The size of the data determines the value and potential insight- and whether it can actually be considered big data or not.

要点概述

（1）体积。指生成数据和存储数据的数量。数据的大小决定了价值和潜在的洞察力，以及它实际上是否可以被认为是大数据。

(2) Variety. The type and nature of the data. This helps people who analyze it to effectively use the resulting insight.

要点概述

（2）种类。数据的类型和性质，这有助于有效地利用由此产生的洞察力。

(3) Velocity. In this context, the speed at which the data is generated and processed to meet the demands and challenges that lie in the path of growth and development.

要点概述

（3）速度。在此背景下指生成和处理数据的速度，以满足增长和发展道路上的需求和挑战。

(4) Variability. Inconsistency of the data set can hamper processes to handle and manage it.

要点概述

（4）易变性。数据集的不一致会阻碍处理和管理数据集的过程。

（5）Veracity. The data quality of captured data can vary greatly, affecting the accurate analysis.

要点概述

（5）准确性。捕获数据的数据质量可以有很大的差异，从而影响准确的分析。

7.2.3 Cross-border e-commerce credit evaluation system based on Big Data

Driven by the economic initiative of "the Silk Road Economic Belt and the 21st Century Maritime Silk Road" (hereinafter referred to as the "B&R"), cross-border e-commerce has recently enjoyed a rapid development, and Big Data has subsequently and officially been promoted as a national agenda. Credit evaluation has always been one of the bottlenecks of cross-border e-commerce development in China. Therefore, it is an irresistible trend to establish credit evaluation system with the application of big data technology.

要点概述

在"丝绸之路经济带和21世纪的海上丝绸之路"的经济倡议推动下，跨境电子商务最近得到迅速发展，大量数据随后正式作为国家议程予以推广。信用评估一直是中国跨境电子商务发展的瓶颈之一。因此，应用大数据技术建立信用评价体系是大势所趋。

An important trend for large data is the change in data services, which divides people into many groups and provides targeted services to each group and even to everyone. The increase of consumption data provides the basis for the electronic business enterprise to accurately grasp the user group and individual network behavior pattern. Through large data application, electric enterprises can explore personalized, individualized, accurate and intelligent advertising push and promotion services, and create a new business model which is more cost-effective than existing advertising and product promotion forms. At the same time, electronic business enterprises can also through the grasp of large data, to find more and better user, the development of new products and services, reduce operating costs of methods and ways. From the domestic point of view, China's electric enterprises are actively in the large data field layout and deep, has gradually recognized the importance of large data applications for the development of the electric business.

要点概述

大数据的重要趋势就是数据服务的变革，把人分成很多群体，对每个群体甚至每个人提供针对性的服务。消费数据量的增加为电商企业提供了精确把握用户群体和个体网络行为模式的基础。电商企业通过大数据应用，可以探索个人化、个性化、精确化和智能化地广告推送和推广服务，创立比现有广告和产品推广形式性价比更高的全新商业模式。同时，电商企业也可以通过对大数据的把握，寻找更多优质客户、增加客户黏性，开发新产品和新服务，降低运营成本的方法和途径。中国电商企业均积极在大数据领域进行布局和深耕，已逐步认识到大数据应用对于电商发展的重要性。

The establishment of cross-border e-commerce credit evaluation system is mainly divided into two parts: credit evaluation index system and credit evaluation model. A well-designed credit evaluation index system is the foundation of building a sufficient credit evaluation system, which calls for rich information from multi-dimensions, multi-levels and multi-channels to constitute original data, from which we can find out the relevance between data and extract indexes that can reflect common characteristics. The hot-spot Big Data technology nowadays is a perfect solution to above-mentioned problems.

要点概述

跨境电子商务信用评价体系的建立主要分为两个部分：信用评价指标体系和信用评价模型。完善的信用评价指标体系是建立充分的信用评价体系的基础，它要求从多维、多层、多渠道等丰富的信息构成原始数据，从中我们可以发现数据和提取索引之间的相关性，这些指标可以反映共同的特征。当今的热点大数据技术是解决以上问题的完美方法。

At present, the two major problems facing China's e-commerce development are cost and homogeneity competition. The arrival of large data age will provide a new way for its development and competition, including specific products and service forms, and enhance the competitiveness of enterprises through personalized innovation. For example, Alibaba through its Taobao, Cat, Aliyun, Alipay, million network and other business platform for resource integration, forming a strong e-commerce customer group and consumer behavior of the whole industry chain information, it created a unique data processing capacity, which is currently other e-commerce companies cannot imitate and follow. At the same time, the competition of e-commerce rises from the simple price war to a level, which forms the competition of differentiation.

要点概述

当前，中国电子商务发展面临的两大突出问题是成本和同质化竞争，而大数据时代的到来将为其发展和竞争提供新的出路，包括具体产品和服务形式，通过个性化创新提升企业竞争力。还是以阿里巴巴为例。阿里巴巴通过对旗下的淘宝、天猫、阿里云、支付宝、万网等业务平台进行资源整合，形成了强大的电子商务客户群及消费者行为的全产业链信息，造就了独一无二的数据处理能力，这是目前其他电子商务公司无法模仿与跟随的。同时，也将电子商务的竞争从简单的价格战上升到一个层次，形成了差异化竞争。

Currently, cross-border e-commerce is enjoying a rapid development as a new trade mode, along with a substantial improvement from quantity to quality. However, due to the uncertainty and lack of credits of both trading parties, the trade risks of cross-border e-commerce are aggravated, which has become one of the major factors in impacting the rapid and healthy development of cross-border e-commerce. It is extremely important to build a complete, ecological and dynamic cross-border e-commerce credit evaluation system and ultimately improve the trading environment, reduce transaction risks and improve trade efficiency. The purpose of establishing a credit system is to establish a "good faith China."

要点概述

目前，跨境电商作为一种新的贸易模式正在迅速发展，从数量到质量都有了很大的改善。然而，由于双方交易双方的不确定性和信用缺失，跨境电商的贸易风险加剧，成为影响跨境电商快速健康发展的主要因素之一。构建一个完整的、生态的和动态的跨境电子商务信用评价体系，并最终改善贸易环境，减少交易风险，提高贸易效率极其重要。建立信用体系的目的是建立一个“诚信的中国”。

The establishment of cross-border e-commerce credit evaluation system of Big Data will certainly generate positive and active influence to our social credit system, comprehensively upgrade the cross-border e-commerce performance of Chinese enterprises, improve the status of Chinese enterprises in international trade, and make remarkable contribution to the economic development of China.

要点概述

跨境电子商务信用评价体系建立的大数据肯定会对我们的社会信用体系产生正面和积极的影响，能全面提升中国企业的跨境电子商务性能，改进中国企业在国际贸易的地位，对中国的经济发展做出显著贡献。

7.3 Cloud computing

7.3.1 Definition

Cloud computing is an information technology (IT) paradigm, a model for enabling ubiquitous access to shared pools of configurable resources (such as computer networks, servers, storage, applications and services), which can be rapidly provisioned with minimal management effort, often over the Internet. Cloud computing allows users and enterprises with various computing capabilities to store and process data either in a privately-owned cloud, or on a third-party server located in a data center, thus making data-accessing mechanisms more efficient and reliable. Cloud computing relies on sharing of resources to achieve coherence and economy of scale, similar to a utility.

要点概述

云计算是一种信息技术（IT）范式，一种用于支持对可配置资源（如计算机网络、服务器、存储、应用程序和服务）的共享池的普遍访问的模型。这些资源可以通过最小的管理工作快速提供，通常是通过 Internet。云计算允许具有各种计算能力的用户和企业在私有云中或位于数据中心的第三方服务器上存储和处理数据，从而使数据访问机制更加有效和可靠。云计算依赖于资源共享来实现一致性和规模经济，类似于一种公用事业。

The term "cloud computing" has been used broadly enough that its definition is accordingly nebulous, but it could be considered simply as a metaphor for the Internet (which is often, appropriately enough, depicted as a cloud in network diagrams). More specifically, cloud computing can be regarded as both an infrastructure and business model, where software and data, rather than being stored locally on your own servers and computers, are delivered to you in real time via the Internet.[5]

5 Newton J. Is Cloud Computing Green Computing?[J]. Gpsolo, 2010.

要点概述

“云计算”一词已被广泛使用，因此它的定义是模糊的，但它可以被简单地看作是互联网的隐喻（它通常是适当的，在网络图中被描述成云）。更具体地说，云计算可以被看作是一个基础设施和商业模式，在那里，软件和数据是通过互联网实时传送给用户的，而不是在本地存储在用户自己的服务器和计算机上。

With the rapid development of the network, enterprise data has been effectively stored at the same time also attracted a lot of viruses and hackers attack, and thus the security of the enterprise data storage is seriously threatened, so that the investment of information security is also getting bigger. By applying cloud computing to the enterprise, you can store data in the cloud, providing professional, efficient, and secure data storage from cloud computing services, so that businesses do not have to worry about data loss because of a variety of security issues. Therefore, cloud computing can provide a reliable and secure data storage center for the enterprise.

要点概述

随着网络的快速发展，企业数据得到有效存储的同时也引来了很多病毒和黑客的攻击，进而使企业数据存储的安全性受到了严重的威胁，使得在信息安全上的投入也越来越大。在企业中应用云计算，可以将数据存储在云端，由云计算服务提供专业、高效和安全的数据存储，从而企业不必再担心由于各种安全问题导致数据丢失。因此，云计算可以为企业提供可靠和安全的数据存储中心。

7.3.2 Cloud computing and environment[6]

Cloud computing and environmentalism are two of the most significant movements of the past decade. Although the two topics are often discussed separately, the ever-increasing impact of information technology on the environment can't be ignored. A recent McKinsey report estimates that IT, as a whole, produces nearly 1 gigaton of emissions a year, accounting for about 2 percent of total global emissions. The world's rapidly increasing demand for computation and data storage will see such emissions increase by the year 2020 to 1.54 gigatons, or 3 percent of global emissions, twice the total output of the United Kingdom today. By some estimates the emissions associated with IT will, by 2020, be greater than those associated with the airline industry. Although the ever-increasing demand for computing cannot be controlled, we must ask if there are ways we can deliver computing in a more efficient, environmentally friendly way. Cloud computing

6 Newton J. Is Cloud Computing Green Computing?[J]. Gpsolo, 2010.

promises such efficiencies, giving rise to the natural question: Can moving more of our computational demands to the cloud help save the environment?

要点概述

云计算和环境保护主义是过去十年中最重要的两个运动。尽管这两个主题经常被单独讨论，但信息技术 (IT) 对环境的影响越来越大，不容忽视。麦肯锡最近的一份报告估计，作为一个整体，它每年产生近 1 gigaton 的排放量，占全球排放总量的大约 2%。世界对计算和数据储存的需求迅速增加，将使这类排放量在 2020 年增至 1.54 t，即全球排放量的 3%，是今天英国总产量的两倍。据估计，到 2020 年，与航空业相关的排放量将会大于航空公司。尽管对计算的需求不断增长，不能控制，但我们必须问，我们是否有办法以更高效、更环保的方式来提供计算。云计算保证了这样的效率，产生了自然的问题：我们可以将更多的计算需求转移到云计算上，从而拯救环境吗？

A large number of computers and network equipment must be equipped for enterprises to build e-commerce systems. It is worth noting that enterprises must periodically replace computers and network equipment in order to meet more and more business needs. The cost of establishing an e-commerce system is relatively high, and higher costs are required in the later stages of development and maintenance. It is difficult for SMEs with relatively limited capital, and it is difficult to match the requirements of fast-growing network services and business applications. . The application of cloud computing in e-commerce can reduce the cost of establishing an enterprise e-commerce system. Enterprises continue to purchase expensive hardware devices through cloud computing, and they also have to pay high maintenance fees. This is mainly because cloud computing can provide IT infrastructure. In this case, only the cloud devices need to be rented. Therefore, cloud computing can provide good economic benefits for the application of enterprise e-commerce.

要点概述

大量的计算机和网络设备是企业构建电子商务系统必须配备的，值得注意的是，企业为了满足越来越多的商务需求，还必须定期对计算机和网络设备进行更换。电子商务系统建立的成本较大，并且开发和维护的后期需要较高的费用，对于资金相对有限的中小企业来讲，是难以承担的，并且与快速成长的网络服务和商务应用要求也难以匹配。云计算在电子商务中的应用能够减少企业电子商务系统的建立成本。企业通过云计算再也不用继续购买昂贵的硬件设备，也不同负担高额的维护费，这主要是云计算能够提供 IT 基础架构，此时只需要租用云端的设备就可以了。由此可见，云计算能够为企业电子商务的应用提供良好的经济效益。

Although the term "cloud computing" evokes an almost ethereal image of an industry with little or no environmental impact, the physical infrastructure running the cloud has a real and growing environmental footprint. The scale of cloud computing data centers is almost hard to imagine. It is said that Google operates more than 1 million servers across three dozen data centers worldwide. Microsoft recently opened a new data center near Chicago that spans more than 500,000 square feet and holds 400,000 servers. The company is adding servers at a rate of 40,000 per month in an effort to catch up with Google. The Smart 2020 report by the Climate Group estimates energy consumption of these and other cloud data centers to be 330 billion kilowatt hours per year.

要点概述

尽管"云计算"一词唤起了几乎没有或没有环境影响的行业的近乎不切实际的形象，但运行云的物理基础设施却有着非常真实且不断增长的环境足迹。云计算数据中心的规模几乎难以想象：据传闻，谷歌在全球 36 个数据中心运营超过 100 万台服务器。微软最近在芝加哥附近开辟了一个新的数据中心，横跨 50 万平方英尺，拥有 40 万台服务器；该公司正在以每月 4 万的速度增加服务器，以努力赶上谷歌。由气候小组发布的智能 2020 报告估计，这些和其他云数据中心的能耗每年为 3300 亿千瓦小时。

7.4 Information and communication technology

7.4.1 Definition

Information and communications technology (ICT) is an extended term for information technology which stresses the role of unified communications and the integration of telecommunications (telephone lines and wireless signals),computers as well as necessary enterprise software, middleware, storage, and audio-visual systems, which enable users to access, store, transmit, and manipulate information. The term ICT is also used to refer to the convergence of audio-visual and telephone networks with computer networks through a single cabling or link system. There are large economic incentives (huge cost savings due to elimination of the telephone network) to merge the telephone network with the computer network system using a single unified system of cabling, signal distribution and management.

要点概述

信息通信技术（ICT）是信息技术的延伸术语，强调通信技术和信息技术（电话线和无线信号）的整合，计算机以及必必要的商业软件，中间件，存储和视听系统这些能够让用户访问，存储，传输和操作信息。信息和通信技术还用于指通过单一布线或链路系统与计算机网络的 audio-visual 和电话网络的汇合。有巨大的经济诱因 (由于取消电话网而节省了巨大的成本) 将电话网络与计算机网络系统合并，使用单一而统一的布线系统、信号分配和管理。

However, ICT has no universal definition, as “the concepts, methods and applications involved in ICT are constantly evolving on an almost daily basis.” The broadness of ICT covers any product that will store, retrieve, manipulate, transmit or receive information electronically in a digital form, e.g. personal computers, digital television, email, robots.

要点概述

然而，信息和通信技术没有统一的定义，因为“涉及信息和通信技术的概念、方法和应用几乎每天都在不断发展”。信息通信技术的宽广包括任何能将存储、检索、操作、传送或接收电子以数字式形式的产品，例如个人计算机、数字式电视、电子邮件、机器人。

On the whole, the rapid development of computer network communication technology provides a powerful guarantee for the use of electronic commerce. With the social development, the application of E-commerce is more and more extensive, cloud computing and E-commerce organic combination is the inevitable trend of future development. With the development of information technology and network communication technology, e-commerce will play a more important role in people's daily life and work, escort people's quality life work.

要点概述

总的来说，计算机网络通信技术迅速发展，为电子商务的使用提供了有力保障。随着社会发展，电子商务应用范围越来越广泛，云计算与电子商务进行有机结合是未来发展的必然趋势。随着信息化技术、网络通信技术的不断发展，电子商务将会在人们的日常生活、工作中起到更加重要的作用，为人们的优质生活工作保驾护航。

7.4.2 ICT development index

The ICT Development Index ranks and compares the level of ICT use and access across the various countries around the world. In 2014 ITU (International Telecommunications Union) released the latest rankings of the IDI, with Denmark attaining the top spot, followed by South Korea. The top 30 countries in the rankings include most high-income countries where quality of life is higher than average, which includes countries from Europe and other regions such as "Australia, Bahrain, Canada, Japan, Macao (China), New Zealand, Singapore and the United States. Almost all countries surveyed improved their IDI ranking this year." The figure shows the size of the netizens.

要点概述

信息和通信技术发展指数是对世界各国信息和通信技术的使用和准入水平的比较和排位。在 2014 年 ITU（国际电信联盟）发布了最新排名，丹麦位列第一，南韩紧随其后。排名前 30 的国家包括大多数高收入国家，那里的生活质量高于平均水平，其中包括来自欧洲和其他地区的国家，如"澳大利亚、巴林、加拿大、日本、澳门（中国）、新西兰、新加坡和美国；几乎所有接受调查的国家都提高了今年的排名。图 7–1 显示的是网民规模。

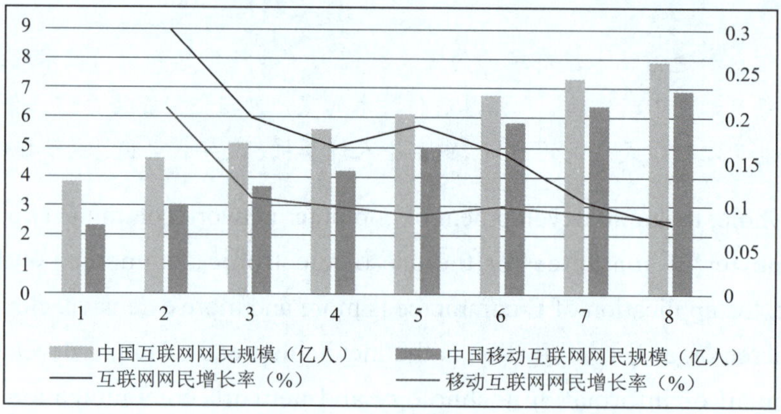

图 7–1　网民规模

In the 2015, cloud computing, Internet of things, large data technology and related industries rapidly rise. A variety of new services flourish, and constantly promote new applications and new industries, promoting the integration of traditional industrial innovation and development. From a cognitive perspective, more than 50% of enterprises are aware of these three new technologies; from the perspective of application, more than 10% of enterprises have adopted, or plan to adopt the relevant technology.

要点概述

在 2015 年，云计算、物联网、大数据技术和相关产业迅速崛起，多种新型服务蓬勃发展，不断催生新应用和新业态，推动传统产业创新融合发展。从认知角度看，超过 50% 的企业对这三类新技术有所知晓；从应用角度看，超过 10% 的企业已经采用、或计划采用相关技术。

Notes:

1. EDI

电子数据交换是企业通过电子方式来传达传统上某些用纸张传达的信息的概念。这类信息的两个典型例子是采购订单和发票。按照同一规定的一套通用标准格式，将标准的经济信息，通过通信网络传输，在贸易伙伴的电子计算机系统之间进行数据交换和自动处理。由于使用 EDI 能有效地减少直到最终消除贸易过程中的纸面单证，因而 EDI 也被俗称为“无纸交易”。它是一种利用计算机进行商务处理的新方法。EDI 是将贸易、运输、保险、银行和海关等行业的信息，用一种国际公认的标准格式，通过计算机通信网络，使各有关部门、公司与企业之间进行数据交换与处理，并完成以贸易为中心的全部业务过程。

2. Big Data

大数据又称为巨量资料，指需要新处理模式才能具有更强的决策力、洞察力和流程优化能力的海量、高增长率和多样化的信息资产。无法在一定时间范围内用常规软件工具进行捕捉、管理和处理的数据集合，是需要新处理模式才能具有更强的决策力、洞察发现力和流程优化能力的海量、高增长率和多样化的信息资产。

3. Cloud computing

云计算是一种信息技术（IT）模式，可以随时访问共享的可配置系统资源池和更高级别的服务。基于互联网的相关服务的增加、使用和交付模式，通常涉及通过互联网来提供动态易扩展且经常是虚拟化的资源。云是网络、互联网的一种比喻说法。过去在图中往往用云来表示电信网，后来也用来表示互联网和底层基础设施的抽象。因此，云计算甚至可以让你体验每秒 10 万亿次的运算能力，拥有这么强大的计算能力可以模拟核爆炸、预测气候变化和市场发展趋势。用户通过电脑、笔记本、手机等方式接入数据中心，按自己的需求进行运算。

4. ICT

信息通信技术（ICT）是信息技术（IT）的延伸术语，强调通信技术和信息技术（电话线和无线信号）的整合，计算机以及必要的商业软件，中间件，存储和视听系统这些能够让用户访问，存储，传输和操作信息。主要反映国内外信息通信技术最新研究成果，提供信息通信技术交流平台，推广先进信息通信业务和应用，为我国建设信息社会和创新型国家服务的刊物。发行主要面向国内外信息通信技术管理机构、运营服务企业、制造企业、大专院校及科研院所的学者、专家、教授、管理者，亦面向信息通信技术领域高新技术企业的一线工程、技术和管理人员。

5. 物联网

物联网是新一代信息技术的重要组成部分，也是“信息化”时代的重要发展阶段。其英文名称是：“Internet of things（IoT）”。顾名思义，物联网就是物物相连的互联网。这有两层意思：其一，物联网的核心和基础仍然是互联网，是在互联网基础上的延伸和扩展的网络；其二，其用户端延伸和扩展到了任何物品与物品之间，进行信息交换和通信，也就是物物相息。物联网通过智能感知、识别技术与普适计算等通信感知技术，广泛应用于网络的融合中，也因此被称为继计算机、互联网之后世界信息产业发展的第三次浪潮。物联网是互联网的应用拓展，与其说物联网是网络，不如说物联网是业务和应用。

Review questions:

According to the topic of this chapter, briefly answer the following questions:

1. What is the specific meaning of EDI and ICT?

2.What are the challenges for companies using electronic data interchange technology?

3. What is the specific meaning of Big Data?

4. What are the components of the cross-border e-commerce credit evaluation system

5. What is the specific meaning of cloud computing?

Chapter 8
Cross-border E-commerce in Hangzhou

8.1 Development status

8.1.1 Institutional mechanism innovation guarantee

On January 28, 2014, Hangzhou municipal party committee and Hangzhou government determined the bonded business settled. Based on the special regulation function of regional policy, they studied the innovation system mechanism, security and integration of advantages of zone resources. A dedicated working group has been established, all departments specialize in the daily work, specially study relevant policies and regulations, innovate and customize business processes, and give full play to the functions of various departments.

要点概述

2014年1月28日，杭州市委、杭州市政府确定保税业务落定，立足于特殊监管区域政策功能，围绕创新体制机制、保障试点运行，整合区内资源优势，进行了探究和研究，建立由招商，综管、海关、检验检疫为核心的工作团队，各部门专人专职参与日常工作，专门研究相关政策法规，创新定制业务流程，充分发挥了各部门的职能作用。

China (Hangzhou) Cross-border E-Commerce Comprehensive Experimental Zone (referred to as "Comprehensive Experimental Zone") realizes cross-border e-commerce information flow, capital flow and cargo flow "three streams in one", through the construction of information sharing system, financial service system, intelligent logistics system, e-commerce credit system, statistical monitoring system and risk prevention and control system, and online "Six-system and two-platform" and "single window" platform and offline "integrated park" platform. Based on this, it is characterized by the organic integration of "free online trading" and "offline comprehensive service", focusing on innovation in "three major areas" such as system construction, government management and service integration. It strives to achieve new breakthroughs in eight areas to achieve cross-border e-commerce liberalization, facilitation and standardization. "Building a new cross-border e-commerce regulatory system, establishing a 'single window' integrated regulatory service platform, innovating cross-border e-commerce financial services, innovating cross-border e-commerce logistics services, innovating cross-border e-commerce credit management, and establishing cross-border e-commerce Statistical monitoring system, development of cross-border e-commerce rules and innovative e-commerce development mechanism, etc."

要点概述

中国（杭州）跨境电子商务综合试验区（简称"综合试验区"）通过构建信息共享体系、金融服务体系、智能物流体系、电商信用体系、统计监测体系和风险防控体系，以及线上"单一窗口"平台和线下"综合园区"平台等"六体系两平台"，实现跨境电子商务信息流、资金流、货物流"三流合一"，并以此为基础，以"线上交易自由"与"线下综合服务"有机融合为特色，重点在制度建设、政府管理、服务集成等"三大领域"开展创新，力争在"建立跨境电子商务新型监管制度、建立'单一窗口'综合监管服务平台、创新跨境电子商务金融服务、创新跨境电子商务物流服务、创新跨境电子商务信用管理、建立跨境电子商务统计监测体系、制定跨境电子商务规则和创新电商人才发展机制"等八个方面实现新突破，实现跨境电子商务自由化、便利化、规范化发展。

8.1.2 Rapid growth in business size

With the cooperation of local e-commerce platform Alibaba Tmall International and Yintai.com cross-border famous products, the development of cross-border trade e-commerce is based on the goal of large-scale normalization. Since the opening of the trade park, Tmall International has carried out a number of trials for thousands of commodities, with an average daily shipment of 5,000. As of the end of November 2014, the cumulative scale reached 800,000, the value of goods reached 1.6.

RMB 100 million, of which 760,000 are in the bonded mode and 38,500 in direct mail, as shown in Table 1.

要点概述

在当地电子商务平台阿里巴巴 T-mall International 与银泰网跨国知名产品的合作下，跨国贸易电子商务的发展是以大规模规范化为目标的。

Since the opening of the trade park, Tmall International has carried out a number of trials for thousands of commodities, with an average daily shipment of 5 000. As of the end of November 2014, the cumulative scale reached 800 000, the value of goods reached 1.6. RMB 100 million, of which 760 000 are in the bonded mode and 38,500 in direct mail, as shown below.

要点概述

自贸易园区开业以来，T-mall 国际公司对数千种商品进行了多次试验，平均每天发货 5 000 件。截至 2014 年 11 月底，累计规模达到 800 000，商品价值达到 1.6，折合人民币 1 亿元，其中保税区 760 000 个，直邮区 38 500 个，如表 8-1 所示。

表 8-1　杭州跨境电子商务产业园工作情况汇报

月份	交易单量	交易值	平均货值	备案企业数	备货数
5 月	3 324	107	321.9	15	500
6 月	18 177	584	321.3	41	1 600
7 月	46 395	1 068	230.2	22	1 200
8 月	79 210	1 693	213.7	25	2 580
9 月	61 189	1 492	243.8	10	2 420

8.1.3 The industrial system is gradually enriched

Through the introduction of a batch of capable, standardized operation projects into the development of the park, Hangzhou cross-border e-commerce related industry system is gradually improving. The main platform includes Alibaba Tmall international, Sinotrans, Netease and other similar electric business platform. There are several vertical electrical business and the professional enterprises to provide technical support for the electricity service and logistics service, such as warehousing software technology, EMS logistics distribution provided by WWWarehouse company. These have paved the way for the industry further agglomeration.

要点概述

通过引入一批有能力，规范操作的项目入园发展，杭州跨境贸易电子商务相关产业体系正在逐步完善。目前主要有天猫国际、中外运、网易等类似的平台电商，还有多家品牌垂直电商以及专业为电商提供技术支持和物流服务的服务性企业，例如，网仓科技提供的仓储技术软件，EMS物流配送等，这些都为产业进一步集聚奠定了基础。

China (Hangzhou) cross-border e-commerce comprehensive experimental zone cracks deep-seated contradictions in the development of cross-border e-commerce through institutional innovation, management innovation, service innovation and coordinated development, and creates a complete industrial chain and ecological chain of cross-border e-commerce. It forms a set of management systems and rules that adapt and lead global cross-border e-commerce development, realizes cross-border e-commerce liberalization, facilitation, and standardized development, and provides reproducible and scalable experience for promoting the healthy development of cross-border e-commerce across the country.

要点概述

中国（杭州）跨境电子商务综合试验区通过制度创新、管理创新、服务创新和协同发展，破解跨境电子商务发展中的深层次矛盾，打造跨境电子商务完整的产业链和生态链，逐步形成一套适应和引领全球跨境电子商务发展的管理制度和规则，实现跨境电子商务自由化、便利化、规范化发展，为推动全国跨境电子商务健康发展提供可复制、可推广的经验。

8.2 Major constraints for cross-border e-commerce in Hangzhou

8.2.1 Policy orientation is unclear

Cross-border e-commerce is a new thing, and various departments and regulations in the country have not yet formulated corresponding policies and regulations. Although Hangzhou, with the strong support of the regulatory authorities, implemented negative inventory management, especially in the inspection and quarantine product list. However, with the advancement of the pilot, various departments have begun to improve the relevant regulations and regulations. Once introduced, the local pilots will form a unified standard, and the operational advantages will also be weakened. Cross-border e-commerce accounts for the market share of e-commerce as shown below.

要点概述

跨境电商是个新事物，全国各部门还没有制定相应的政策法规，各个都是试点城市，虽然杭州属地在监管部门的大力支持下，执行了负面清单管理，尤其是检验检疫产品清单等方面比较领先，抢占了发展先机，但随着试点的推进，各个部门已经着手健全相关法规规定，一旦出台，各地试点将统一形成标准，操作优势也将减弱。2018—2017 年中国跨境电商占电商市场份额如图 8-1 所示。

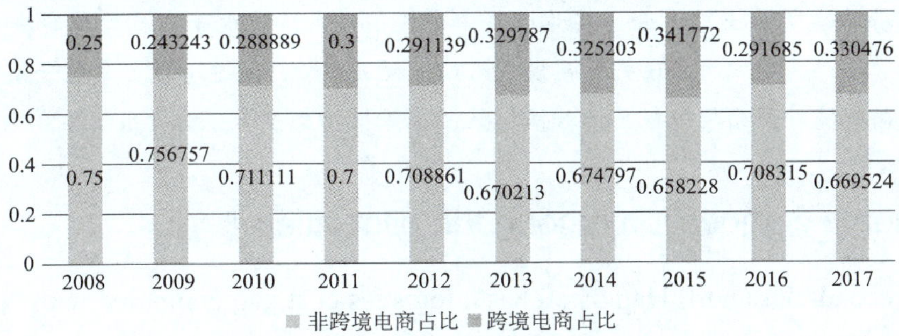

图 8-1 2008—2017 年中国跨境电商占电商市场份额

8.2.2 Regulation and staffing cannot meet the needs

With the continuous entry of many high-quality e-commerce companies, the scale of Hangzhou cross-border trade e-commerce industrial park business continues to expand. During the experience of Alibaba Tmall International Double 11, there were serious shortages of supervisors, especially customs and inspection and quarantine personnel. It is necessary to gradually explore the regulatory principles and operational procedures of the business in practice. Local governments also strengthen innovative thinking and improve their supervisory capabilities in terms of increasing personnel and improving operational efficiency, thus adapting to regulatory needs.

要点概述

随着很多优质电商的不断入驻，杭州跨境贸易电子商务产业园的业务规模不断扩大。尤其在阿里巴巴天猫国际双 11 期间，出现监管人员的严重不足，特别是海关和检验检疫人员的不足。因此，在实践中逐渐探索出该业务的监管原则和操作流程是必要的，地方政府也应加强创新思维，从增加人员和提高操作效率两方面来提高监管能力，从而适应监管需求。

Hangzhou cross-border trade e-commerce service platform mainly serves small-scale cross-border e-commerce export business, taking into account imports. In terms of e-commerce cross-border trade exports, it implements a “centralized declaration” model to integrate e-commerce cross-border trade into general trade cargo management. The import customs clearance business model is "bonded import". Through cross-border trade e-commerce platform, overseas sellers will declare foreign goods into the bonded area and declare them in the bonded logistics center in batches.

要点概述

杭州跨境贸易电子商务服务平台以服务小额跨境电子商务出口业务为主，兼顾进口。在电子商务跨境贸易出口方面，实施"集中申报"模式，将电子商务跨境贸易纳入一般贸易货物管理；进口方面的通关业务模式为"保税进口"，通过跨境贸易电子商务平台，境外销售商将境外商品集中报关进入保税区，在保税物流中心分批申报出区。

8.2.3 Fierce competition among the pilot cities

As a second-class port, Hangzhou has a logistics cost gap compared with Ningbo and Guangzhou. On the other hand, competition in the same city also diverts many resource advantages. It is necessary to carefully analyze regional advantages, achieve resource integration and mutual learning, and thus achieve characteristic development.

要点概述

杭州作为二类口岸，与宁波、广州等地存在物流成本差距；另一方面，同城竞争也分流了很多资源优势。需要认真分析区域优势，做到资源整合、相互学习，从而实现特色化发展。

Technical innovation ability of export commodities: mainly in clothing and cosmetics, the proportion of capital-intensive products is very small.

要点概述

出口商品技术创新能力：以服装和化妆品为主，资本密集型产品比重很小。

At present, Hangzhou's cross-border e-commerce export commodities are mainly clothing and cosmetics, accounting for 55% and 32.5% of their total exports, respectively, and the overall proportion is nearly 90%. Mechanical manufacturing products account for only 5%. In general, the technical content of services and cosmetics is not high, and the technical complexity is not strong, and services and cosmetics can be attributed to labor-intensive simple manufacturing products. Mechanical manufacturing goods are capital-intensive products, representing a strong technological innovation capability, but they account for a small proportion of cross-border e-commerce export trade.

要点概述

目前，杭州跨境电商出口商品以服装和化妆品为主，分别占到其出口总量的55%和32.5%，总体比重将近90%；机械制造产品比重仅占5%。一般而言，服务和化妆品的技术含量不高，技术复杂度也不强，可以归属于劳动密集型的简单制造商品，而机械制造商品是资本密集型产品，代表了较强的技术创新能力，但是，在跨境电商出口贸易所占比重较小。

Export target market expansion capacity: mainly developed countries in Europe and the United States, emerging markets need to expand.

要点概述

出口目标市场拓展能力：以欧美发达国家为主，新兴市场有待拓展。

At present, Hangzhou's main export target market for cross-border e-commerce is concentrated in the developed countries in Europe and the United States, accounting for 67.5% and 50% respectively, followed by Asian countries, accounting for 37.5%, while Latin American countries accounted for only 5%. It is true that the dependence of cross-border e-commerce in Hangzhou on developed countries in Europe and America is still relatively high, and the Asian market and Latin American market under the influence of the "One Belt, One Road" development strategy also have great development potential. Most of the interviewed business leaders said that the developed markets of the United States, the United Kingdom, Germany, Australia, and Canada are relatively mature, with early-mover advantages such as relatively strong consumer demand, strong cross-border online shopping awareness, and logistics facilities.

要点概述

目前，杭州跨境电商主要出口目标市场集中在欧美发达国家，占比分别达到67.5%和50%；其次是亚洲国家，占比达到37.5%；而拉美国家占比只有5%。诚然，杭州跨境电商对欧美发达国家的依赖性还比较高，而"一带一路"倡议影响下的亚洲市场和拉美市场还具有较大的开发潜力。大多访谈企业负责人都表示，以美国、英国、德国、澳大利亚、加拿大为代表的欧美发达国家的市场比较成熟，具有消费需求相对旺盛、跨境网购意识强、物流配套设施等先发市场优势。

8.3 Suggestions on the further development

8.3.1 Improve business scale and logistics efficiency

On the basis of serving well-established enterprises, Hangzhou cross-border trade e-commerce strives for more business to enter the park, guarantees the simultaneous development of bonded import and direct mail import, and guides e-commerce products to high-end and diversified development. At the same time, the protection of all personnel is in place, and customs and inspection and quarantine personnel can improve their supervision capabilities in terms of increasing personnel and improving operational efficiency, thus adapting to regulatory needs.

要点概述

杭州跨境贸易电子商务在服务好现有入驻企业的同时，争取更多的业务入园，实现保税进口和直邮进口同步发展，引导电商产品向高端化。多元化发展。同时各人员保障到位，海关和检验检疫人员从增加人员和提高操作效率两方面来提高监管能力，从而适应监管需求。

8.3.2 Vigorously promote and expand the influence of pilot

While promoting its influence, Hangzhou cross-border trade e-commerce pilots should attract the attention of all parts of the country and vigorously promote the standardization of its own advantages, such as the standardization of data docking and the whole process of order information, payment information and logistics information. Further measures should be taken to attract customer experience and to gather cross-border trade e-commerce enterprises.

要点概述

杭州跨境贸易电子商务试点在提升自己影响力的同时，更应该吸引全国各地的关注，大力宣传自身优势，例如，数据对接的规范化操作和订单信息、支付信息、物流信息的全程监管。在吸引客户体验力度和集聚跨境贸易电子商务企业力度方面，应采取进一步的措施。

8.3.3 Explore cross-border trade export business

Cross-border e-commerce export business has been very active, and the main products for export are household, clothing, luggage and auto parts. Hangzhou has the Sijiqing clothing trading market, which is inexpensive, chooses high-quality goods, inspects the needs of the international market, selects pilot enterprises, and conducts export trade. At the same time, Hangzhou also has many famous brands such as small household appliances, home, shoes, hats and cosmetics. Relevant products and screening pilot export enterprises, and then appropriate training, make full use of the existing platform to carry out export business. While insisting on making full use of existing resources, we must adhere to the principle of equal emphasis on export and import and develop together.

要点概述

跨境电子商务出口业务一直也在十分火热地进行，出口的主要热门产品是家居类、服装类、箱包类和汽配类等。杭州拥有四季青服装交易市场，物美价廉，选择优质的商品，考察国际市场的需求，选择试点企业，进行出口贸易；同时杭州也拥有很多小家电、家居、鞋帽、化妆品等著名品牌，选择相关类产品以及筛选试点出口企业，再进行适当培训，充分利用现有平台，开展出口业务。在坚持充分利用现有资源的同时，坚持出口和进口并重原则，共同发展。

Notes:

1. EMS

邮政特快专递服务。它是由万国邮联管理下的国际邮件快递服务，公司全国员工近万人，EMS 业务包括国内所有市县，延伸亚洲地区，EMS 是中国邮政提供的一种快递服务。

2. SINOTRANS

中外运是国内航空货运代理行业第一家上市公司，核心业务包括航空货运代理、速递及综合物流，其中国际货运代理业务稳居国内行业第一，成立于 1999 年 10 月，并于 2000 年 12 月 28 日在上海证券交易所成功上市。

Review questions:

According to the topic of this chapter, briefly answer the following questions:

(1) What is the related industrial system of the e-commerce of Hangzhou cross-border trade？

(2) What are the problems and solutions in the electronic commerce industry of Hangzhou’s cross-border trade?

Chapter 9

Cross-border E-commerce in Chongqing

9.1 Development status

Chongqing has become one of the first pilot cities of Cross-border e-commerce services for national trade. After two or three years of development, Chongqing's Cross-border e-commerce transaction volume leaps and bounds, and Cross-border electrical business transactions related services are improving.

要点概述

重庆市成为首批国家跨境贸易电子商务服务试点城市之一。经过两三年的发展，重庆的跨境电子商务交易额突飞猛进，跨境电商交易相关服务日臻完善。

Cross-border e-commerce is an innovative foreign trade business model. The development of cross-border e-commerce in Chongqing is significant, and plays a leading role in the development of international trade in China's western regions. This paper puts forward some countermeasures in view of the problems existing in the development of cross-border electronic commerce in Chongqing: third-party credit institutions and buyers and sellers of cross-border e-commerce cooperate with relevant departments to strengthen supervision and improve the credit system; make full use of the "Belt and Road" initiative to strengthen financial guidance for cross-border e-commerce development; relevant departments establish and improve cross-border third parties Payment supervision system; universities, enterprises and government combine to build a new talent training model.

要点概述

跨境电子商务是一种创新型外贸商业模式，重庆跨境电子商务发展成绩可观，并在中国西部地区国际贸易发展中起领头作用。本文针对重庆跨境电子商务发展中存在的问题提出相应对策：第三方信用机构和跨境电子商务的买卖方配合相关部门加强监管并完善信用体系；充分利用好“一带一路”倡议以加强金融引导跨境电子商务的发展；相关部门建立和完善跨境第三方支付监管体系；高校、企业和政府三方面结合，构建新型人才培养模式。

9.1.1 The exponential growth of cross-border e-commerce trading

In order to promote the development of cross-border e-commerce in Chongqing, the integrated service platform of Cross-border e-commerce was launched in January 2014. According to statistics, in 2014, Chongqing cross-border e-commerce volume are 66.3672 million yuan. In 2015, the Chongqing cross-border e-commerce turnover was nearly 1 billion yuan; In 2016, turnover has exceeded 14 billion yuan. Chongqing cross-border e-commerce into the rapid development period. In 2017, the formation of a development system and comprehensive security system, the formation of a cross-border e-commerce industry-specific system, the realization of cross-border e-commerce total of 10 billion U.S. dollars.

要点概述

为了推动重庆跨境电商发展，跨境贸易电子商务综合服务平台于 2014 年 1 月上线运行。据统计，2014 年，重庆市跨境电商交易额 6636.72 万元。2015 年，重庆市跨境电商交易额近 10 亿元。2016 年，交易额已突破 140 亿元。重庆跨境电商进入高速发展时期。到 2017 年，形成适应跨境电子商务发展的体制机制和综合保障体系，形成具有内陆特色的跨境电子商务产业体系，实现跨境电子商务总额 100 亿美元。

9.1.2 Cross-border logistics

In order to deliver products to foreign customers at low cost, the cross-border logistics channel of Chongqing has achieved certain results with the joint efforts of the government and cross-border e-commerce companies. Overseas warehouses have become bridgeheads for cross-border e-commerce export enterprises. Free trade zones, bonded zones and bonded warehouses have become the best solution for cross-border import of e-commerce logistics.

要点概述

跨境电商的发展，需要强大的物流系统的支撑。为了低成本地将产品送达异国客户手中，在政府和跨境电商企业的共同努力下，重庆市的跨境物流通道取得了一定的成效。海外仓成为跨境电商出口企业的桥头堡，自贸区、保税区及保税仓成为跨境进口电商物流的最佳解决方案。

Since 2013, Chongqing has become one of the first "pilot cities for Cross-border Electric Service", and cross-border e-commerce has become a new direction of foreign trade growth in Chongqing. It is reported that 2014 Chongqing Cross-border Trade Electronic Services pilot Cumulative total order amount of 227,000 orders, the total business volume of 66.3672 million yuan. The import list that Chongqing Customs inspected and released in 2015 was 3,326,900, a year-on-year increase of 14.9 times, and the total trade volume was 786 million yuan, a year-on-year increase of 12.1 times. The scale of Cross-border e-commerce business in Chongqing is increasing every year, and the proportion of the total business scale of China's trans-boundary E-commerce is increasing every year. In 2015, the total import of Cross-border E-commerce in Chongqing amounted to 785 million yuan, exports amounted to 395 million U.S. dollars. The total import and export volume of Chongqing in January-April 2016 was 1.59 times that of the whole year of 2015.

要点概述

重庆自 2013 年成为全国首批"跨境电商服务试点城市"之一以来，跨境电子商务成为促进重庆外贸增长的新方向。据报道，2014 年重庆跨境贸易电子服务试点累计完成订单量共计 22.7 万单，总业务额达 6 636.72 万元，重庆海关在 2015 年检验并放行的进口清单有 332.69 万单，同比增长了 14.9 倍左右，总贸易额 7.86 亿元，同比增长了 12.1 倍多。重庆跨境电子商务业务规模正在逐年上升，占中国跨境电子商务总业务规模的比例也在逐年上升，2015 年重庆市跨境电子商务进口总额为 7.85 亿元，出口总额为 3.95 亿美元，2016 年 1～4 月重庆市进出口总额是 2015 年全年的 1.59 倍。

9.1.3 Customs supervision mode

Due to the particularity of cross-border e-commerce products, the relevant authorities have issued corresponding policies to protect the development of cross-border e-commerce, so that the people of Chongqing can achieve "buy the world and sell the world". Chongqing customs changes its thinking mode to explore new ways of cross-border e-commerce supervision, speed up cross-border e-commerce customs clearance, reduce customs clearance costs, and achieve better development of cross-border e-commerce business.

要点概述

由于跨境电商产品的特殊性，相关主管单位出台相应政策为跨境电商发展保驾护航，从而让重庆人民实现“买全球、卖全球”。重庆海关转变思维模式探索出跨境电商监管新办法，加快跨境电商通关速度，降低通关成本，实现跨境电商业务更好地发展。

9.2 Analysis of existing problems

9.2.1 Cross-border logistics restricts the development of cross-border e-commerce

Cross-border logistics costs, transport time, return and exchange problems have seriously restricted the development of cross-border e-commerce. “Yu-Xin-Ou” Railway main carrier IT products, cross-border e-commerce products accounted for a low proportion. At present, these temperature-controlled goods are mainly transported by sea refrigerated containers to Chongqing, a small part of the use of air transport methods.

要点概述

跨境物流成本、运输时间、退换货等问题已经严重制约了跨境电子商务的发展。“渝新欧”铁路主要承运的 IT 产品、跨境电子商务产品所占比例较低。目前，这些温控货物主要是通过海运冷藏集装箱运往重庆，小部分使用空运方式。

The transportation cost of the marine refrigerated box is high, the time is long, the cold chain air transport has the actual effect superiority, but has the limitation which the cost is high, the batch is limited. In addition, for the small and medium cross-boundary electric power business enterprises, in the current “Chongqing and New Europe” volume (including international mail) has not yet formed the scale of the background, more use of sea and even air transport logistics solutions.

要点概述

海运冷藏箱运输成本高、时间长，冷链空运具有实效优势，但也有成本高、批次有限的局限性。另外，对于中小型跨境电商企业而言，在目前“重庆和新欧洲”的货量（包括国际邮件）还没有形成规模的背景下，更多地采用海运乃至空运的物流解决方案。

The “Yu-Xin-Ou” railway cannot meet the needs of cross-border e-commerce products on hardware equipment. Imports of goods such as red wine, meat, dairy products and fruit fresh foods require cold chain transport, and the "Yu-Xin-Ou" railway does not currently have such equipment.

要点概述

"渝新欧"铁路在硬件设备上不能满足跨境电商商品的需要。如红酒、肉类、奶制品和水果生鲜食品等货品的进口就需要冷链运输，而"渝新欧"现在还没有这类设备。

9.2.2 Regulatory standards still need to be improved

During the launch of the cross-border e-commerce transaction service platform in Chongqing, 559 online shopping complaints were accepted. False delivery, false promotions, false publicity, false exemptions, price fraud, shipping issues, quality issues, after-sales service, and refunds have become the top nine promotion issues this year. From these aspects, it can be seen that cross-border e-commerce platforms need to increase supervision to reduce the complaint rate and improve customer service levels.

要点概述

重庆跨境电子商务交易服务平台上线期间，受理的网购投诉达559件。虚假发货、虚假促销、虚假宣传、虚假免单、价格欺诈、发货问题、质量问题、售后服务、退款问题成为今年的九大问题。从这些方面可以看出跨境电商平台需要加大监管力度，以降低投诉率提高顾客服务水平。

Trading credit is more important for businesses engaged in cross-border e-commerce. According to the survey, there were 559 online shopping complaints in Chongqing in 2014 and 562 in 2015, up 0.7% and 0.4% respectively. China has no specific norms and standards for transactions, taxes, and consumer rights protection involved in cross-border e-commerce. There are false propaganda, illegal transactions, sales of counterfeit and shoddy products, fraudulent acts and infringement of intellectual property rights in Chongqing's cross-border e-commerce platform.

要点概述

交易信用对于从事跨境电子商务的商家更为重要。据调查显示，2014年重庆市的网购投诉达559件，2015年为562件，同比分别增长0.7%和0.4%。我国对于跨境电子商务所涉及的交易、税收以及消费者权益保护方面并没有具体规范和标准。重庆跨境电子商务平台中存在虚假宣传、非法交易、销售假冒伪劣产品、欺诈行为以及侵犯知识产权等行为。

9.2.3 Shortage of talents

At present, there is no special cross-border e-commerce major in Chongqing or even universities across the country. Cross-border e-commerce talents are either from international economics and trade, or from e-commerce. High-end operational talents who have both foreign language communication and communication skills and Internet thinking and technology are extremely scarce. Cross-border e-commerce has the characteristics of strong practical ability and fast knowledge update, and the growth of its talents requires the accumulation of long-term practical experience. However, the local foreign trade enterprises in Chongqing started the cross-border e-commerce late, and the foreign language level and e-commerce skills of the practitioners were uneven. It is difficult to conduct foreign trade business through the network platform.

要点概述

目前，重庆乃至全国的高校均未开设跨境电子商务专业，跨境电商人才来自国际经济与贸易，或电子商务专业。既掌握外语交流及沟通能力又具有互联网思维与技术的高端运营人才极度匮乏。跨境电商有实践能力强、知识更新快的特点，其人才的成长需要长期实践经验的积累，而重庆本地外贸企业开展跨境电商起步较晚，从业者外语水平和电子商务技能参差不齐，通过网络平台开展外贸业务较为困难。

9.3 Related recommendations

9.3.1 Give full play to the advantages of location

Chongqing is located at the junction of the Belt and Road, connecting the east and the west, and the north and the south, with obvious location advantages. There are 26 countries along the "Belt and Road", covering a population of 4.4 billion, accounting for about 63% of the world. The economic scale is 21 trillion US dollars, accounting for 29% of the global market. The demand for cross-border e-commerce market is relatively large. Therefore, Chongqing should make full use of its location advantages, thoroughly study the market demand of the "Belt and Road" countries, and actively develop cross-border e-commerce. Chongqing's cross-border e-commerce, an emerging industry, plays an important role in the construction of the "Belt and Road", and financial services should provide guidance and assistance. To give full play to the role of financial guidance in promoting cross-border e-commerce in Chongqing, we must use the "Belt and Road" to attract investment financing. We should strengthen monetary cooperation and promote the internationalization of the RMB. Encouraging the use of RMB for payment settlement may not be realized at present, but China's comprehensive strength is constantly developing and it is still possible to achieve it in the future. In the case of ensuring security, it is necessary to strengthen the understanding of cross-border e-commerce by investment companies or individuals, establish relevant credit insurance institutions, and work with countries around the world to crack down on regional financial crime activities.

要点概述

重庆地处一带一路连接点，承东启西、连接南北，特殊区位优势明显。“一带一路”沿线26个国家，覆盖人口44亿左右，约占全球的63%。经济规模21万亿美元，约占全球的29%，跨境电商市场需求比较大，所以重庆市应充分利用自身区位优势，深入研究“一带一路”国家市场需求，积极发展跨境电商。重庆跨境电子商务这一新兴产业对“一带一路”建设具有重要作用，金融服务应在其中给予引导帮助。充分发挥金融引导对重庆跨境电商的促进作用，就要借助“一带一路”吸引投资融资。应该加强货币合作，推进人民币国际化，使用人民币进行支付结算在目前或许还不能实现，但中国综合实力不断发展，在未来还是有可能实现的。在确保安全性的情况下，应加强投资企业或个人对于跨境电子商务的理解，建立相关信用保险机构，同时与世界各国合力对区域金融犯罪活动进行打击。

9.3.2 Strengthen the supply chain construction of cross-border e-commerce

The integration of supply chain into the development trend of modern cross-border e-commerce is a time when many giants are laying the cross-border e-commerce. Chongqing cross-border e-business enterprises should actively communicate with suppliers, channel providers and customers, technology sharing, strengthen supply chain construction, provide quality service to customers and improve customer satisfaction.

要点概述

供应链融入现代跨境电子商务的发展趋势，是众多巨头纷纷为跨国电子商务铺垫的时代。重庆跨境电子商务企业应积极与供应商、渠道供应商和客户沟通，技术共享，加强供应链建设，为客户提供优质服务，提高客户满意度。

To improve cross-border e-commerce logistics, we need to start with transportation, inspection, customs clearance and warehousing. The establishment of two bonded areas in Chongqing and the operation of the “Yu-Xin-Ou” international railway channel have provided more convenient logistics services for the development of cross-border e-commerce in Chongqing. In addition, in order to ensure more efficient services for cross-border e-commerce logistics, foreign trade enterprises may consider adopting third-party warehousing modes such as overseas warehouses in countries where transactions are better.

要点概述

改善跨境电商物流，需从运输、报检、通关、仓储几个环节入手。重庆两个保税区的建立和“渝新欧”国际铁路大通道的运行为重庆跨境电商的发展提供了更加便利的物流服务。另外，为保证跨境电子商务物流更加高效地提供服务，外贸企业可考虑在交易较好的所在国采用第三方仓储模式，如海外仓等。

9.3.3 Strengthen the supervision of cross-border e-commerce market

Although cross-border e-commerce has a good development prospect, the legal system for cross-border e-commerce has not yet been introduced. Therefore, it is recommended that a special department be established to supervise cross-border platforms in the form of irregular inspections, regular spot checks, special education and publicity at any time. In addition, it is also possible to introduce corresponding regulations and regulations to punish illegal cross-border e-commerce enterprises in order to create a harmonious, standardized and orderly cross-border e-commerce operation environment.

要点概述

虽然跨境电商具有良好的发展前途，但是有关跨境电商方面的法律体系还未出台。因此，建议可以设立专门的部门，采取不定期检查、定期抽查、专题教育以及随时宣传的形式对跨境平台进行监管。此外，还可以出台相应的法规条例对违规跨境电商企业进行惩罚，以便营造一种和谐、规范、有序的跨境电商运营环境。

In order to standardize the payment of cross-border e-commerce in Chongqing, we should vigorously promote the Chongqing payment institution to carry out the overseas payment pilot work, and allow the pilot payment institutions to handle overseas receipts and disbursements and exchange transactions. At the same time, in line with the facilitation of financial guidance, we should actively promote cross-border e-commerce activities RMB International Settlement, support domestic bank card clearing institutions to carry out overseas business, strengthen the research and application of information security technology, guarantee the security and stability of the payment system, guard against the risks caused by Internet security accidents and technical problems, support Third-party payment agencies to carry out cross-border payment operations, and expand cross-border payment market share. Chongqing Foreign Exchange Supervision Department should take the business supervision as the basic criterion, make efforts to do research, look for the risk point, formulate the specific and operable supervision measures.

要点概述

为规范重庆跨境电子商务支付，应大力推进重庆支付机构开展境外支付试点工作，允许试点支付机构办理境外收支和外汇交易。同时，根据金融引导的便利，积极推进跨境电子商务活动人民币国际结算，支持国内银行卡结算机构开展国内银行卡结算业务。拓展海外业务，加强信息安全技术的研究和应用，保障支付系统的安全性和稳定性，防范网络安全事故和技术问题带来的风险。

9.3.4 Strengthen the introduction and cultivation of cross-border e-commerce talents

With the approval of China's Chongqing Free Trade Zone, Chongqing is short of a large number of compound talents who understand foreign trade, English, and e-commerce operations management. Chongqing municipality can do a good job in cross-border e-commerce talents training through joint training of schools and enterprises, training and introduction of third-party institutions.

要点概述

随着中国重庆自贸区的获批，重庆急缺一大批既懂外贸、英语，又懂电商运营管理的复合型人才。重庆市可通过校企联合培养、第三方机构培训、引进等方式做好跨境电商人才培养。

Chongqing has introduced the experience of cross-border e-commerce talents in the coastal areas while attaching importance to the cultivation of local talents. The construction of a new talent training model requires the division of labor, cooperation between universities, enterprises and the government. All colleges and universities in Chongqing should build a practical teaching system and effectively innovate the business training model of cross-border e-commerce. Enterprises should do a good job in human resource planning, divide talent levels, give employees promotion space, mobilize the enthusiasm of talents at all levels, increase the welfare of high-level cross-border e-commerce professionals, and establish and improve incentive mechanisms for personnel training.

要点概述

重庆在引进沿海地区经验丰富的跨境电子商务人才的同时，重视对本土人才的培养。新型人才培养模式的构建需要高校、企业和政府三方面分工合作。重庆各高校应建设好实践性教学体系，对跨境电子商务的业务培训模式进行有效创新。企业应做好人力资源规划，划分人才层次，给予员工晋升空间，调动各层次人才的发展积极性，增加高层次跨境电子商务专业人才的福利，建立并完善人才培养相关方面的激励机制。

Notes:

1. 海外仓

海外仓指企业按照一般贸易方式，将商品批量出口到境外仓库，拿到订单后，再将商品送达境外的客户及消费者。在除本国地区的其他国家建立的海外仓库，一般用于电子商务。货物从本国出口通过海运、货运、空运的形式储存到该国的仓库，买家通过网上下单购买所需物品，卖家只需在网上操作，对海外的仓库下达指令完成订单履行。货物从买家所在国发出，大大缩短了从本国发货物流所需要的时间。

2. 国际快递

国际快递是指在两个或两个以上国家（或地区）之间所进行的快递、物流业务。国家与国家（或地区）传递信函、商业文件及物品的递送业务，即是通过国家之间的边境口岸和海关对快件进行检验放行的运送方式。国际快件到达目的国家之后，需要在目的国进行再次转运，才能将快件送达最终目的地。

3. 供应链

供应链的概念是从扩大的生产（Extended Production）概念发展而来，供应链是围绕核心企业，从配套零件开始到制成中间产品及最终产品、最后由销售网络把产品送到消费者手中的一个由供应商、制造商、分销商直到最终用户所连成的整体功能网链结构。供应链管理的经营理念是从消费者的角度，通过企业间的协作，谋求供应链整体最佳化。

Review questions:

According to the topic of this chapter, briefly answer the following questions:

(1) What is the development status of Chongqing e-commerce platform?

(2) What are the problems of the Cross-border e-commerce platform in Chongqing?

(3) What are the solutions of the Cross-border e-commerce platform in Chongqing?

Chapter 10

Threats and Challenges

10.1 Customs formality, legal and regulatory issues

10.1.1 Customs formality

Customs is an authority or agency in a country responsible for collecting tariffs and for controlling the flow of goods, including animals, transports, personal, and hazardous items, into and out of a country. The movement of people into and out of a country is normally monitored by immigration authorities, under a variety of names and arrangements. The immigration authorities normally check for appropriate documentation, verify that a person is entitled to enter the country, apprehend people wanted by domestic or international arrest warrants, and impede the entry of people deemed dangerous to the country. In many places, K9 units are also used.

要点概述

海关是一国负责征收关税和控制货物流（包括动物、运输、个人和危险物品）进出的当局或机构。进出一国的人员流动通常由移民当局以各种名义和安排加以监测。移民当局通常检查合法证件，核实某人是否有权进入该国，逮捕国内或国际逮捕令所通缉的人，并阻止被认为对该国有危险的人入境。在许多地方，也被称之为K9。

The political and economic conditions of different countries are different, and customs duties are also different. Even in the same country, customs duties have changed in various historical periods. However, several duties such as customs clearance, tariffs and other taxes, and smuggling are basically the same for most countries.

要点概述

各国政治、经济情况不尽相同，海关职责也有差异，即使同一国家，各个历史时期海关职责也有变化。但是，通关管理、征收关税和其他税费、缉查走私等几项职责是绝大多数国家海关基本相同的。

According to the Customs Law of the People's Republic of China, there are four functions of China's customs: supervision, taxation, private investigation and preparation of customs statistics.

要点概述

根据《中华人民共和国海关法》规定，中国海关职能有 4 项：监管、征税、查私和编制海关统计。

10.1.2 Legal and regulatory issues

Each country has its own laws and regulations for the import and export of goods into and out of a country, which its customs authority enforces. The import or export of some goods may be restricted or forbidden. In most countries, customs are attained through government agreements and international laws. A customs duty is a tariff or tax on the importation (usually) or exportation (unusually) of goods. Commercial goods not yet cleared through customs are held in a customs area, often called a bonded store, until processed. All authorized ports are recognized customs areas.

要点概述

每个国家都有自己的关于进出口货物进出一个国家的法律和条例，由其海关当局强制执行。某些货物的进出口可能受到限制或禁止。在大多数国家，关税通过政府协定和国际法获得。海关税收是对进口（通常）或出口（不寻常）货物征收的关税或税。尚未通关的商品，通常被关在海关区域，通常被称为保税店，直到处理完毕。所有授权的港口都是公认的海关区域。

Because small-scale B2B and B2C cross-border trade e-commerce is different from general export trade, it is difficult to quickly clear customs, regulate foreign exchange settlement, and enjoy tax rebate in the export process. Although the current state proposes a customs clearance model for cross-border e-commerce retail exports that can be "listed for nuclear release and summary declaration", the policy is only for B2C enterprises, and a large number of foreign trade small and medium-sized enterprises engaged in small B2B still have difficulties in customs clearance. In the process of importing, there are problems such as evading customs supervision by illegal import channels, and the quality of imported goods is difficult to identify, and consumer rights are not guaranteed.

要点概述

由于小额 B2B 和 B2C 跨境贸易电子商务与一般出口贸易有差异，在出口过程中存在难以快速通关、规范结汇、享受退税等问题，虽然目前国家针对跨境电商零售出口提出“清单核放、汇总申报”的通关模式，但该政策仅针对 B2C 企业，大量从事小额 B2B 的外贸中小企业仍存在通关困难的问题。在进口过程中，存在以非法进口渠道逃避海关监管，以及进口商品品质难以鉴别，消费者权益得不到保障等问题。

10.2 Online Dispute Resolution

10.2.1 Introduction

Online dispute resolution (ODR) is a branch of dispute resolution which uses technology to facilitate the resolution of disputes between parties. In this respect it is often seen as being the online equivalent of alternative dispute resolution (ADR).

要点概述

在线纠纷解决是纠纷解决的一个分支，它利用技术来促进当事人之间纠纷的解决。在这方面，它经常被视为在线替代纠纷解决机制（ADR）。

10.2.2 Online dispute resolution procedure

Dispute resolution techniques range from methods where parties have full control of the procedure, to methods where a third party is in control of both the process and the outcome. These primary methods of resolving disputes may be complemented with Information and Communication Technology (ICT). When the process is conducted mainly online it is referred to as ODR, i.e. to carry out most of the dispute resolution procedure online, including the initial filing, the neutral appointment, evidentiary processes, oral hearings if needed, online discussions. Thus, ODR is a different medium to resolve disputes.

要点概述

争端解决技术从当事方完全控制程序，到第三方同时控制过程和结果的方法不一而足。这些解决争端的主要方法可辅之以信息和通信技术(ICT)。当这一程序主要在网上进行时，称为ODR，即在网上执行大多数争议解决程序，包括初次备案、中立任命、举证程序、必要时的口头听证以及在线讨论。因此，ODR是解决争端的另一种媒介。

It is believed that efficient mechanisms to resolve online disputes will impact in the development of e-commerce. The ODR does not have a fixed meaning and scope, which includes the methods and modes of solving the various disputes of B2C e-commerce in the global e-commerce environment.

要点概述

人们相信，有效解决网上纠纷的机制将对电子商务的发展产生影响。ODR没有固定的含义和范围，其包括了全球电子商务环境下解决各种B2C电商纠纷的方法和模式。

It embodies the principle of party autonomy to the greatest extent. It has the characteristics of dispute resolution and applicable rules, the efficiency of dispute processing, and the economics of dispute resolution (low cost). Online mediation and online arbitration are the most common online dispute resolution methods.

要点概述

在线争议处理机制最大程度上体现了当事人意思自治原则，具有纠纷解决方式和适用规则的灵活性、争端处理的高效性、纠纷解决的经济性（低费用）等特点。

The basic principle of online mediation is the same as traditional mediation. The difference is that the entire process of mediation is carried out on the network. The characteristics of online mediation are:

要点概述

在线调解和在线仲裁是最常见的在线争端解决方式。在线调解的基本原理同传统调解一样，不同的是调解的全部过程在网络上进行。在线调解的特点是：

(1) It is more representative of the willingness of the parties. The parties are free to decide whether to adopt such a method, or they are free to decide whether to participate in the procedure;

要点概述

（1）更能体现当事人的自我意愿。当事人可以自由决定是否采取该种方式，也可以自由决定是否参与到程序中；

(2) their procedures are less constrained by legal norms. In online mediation, a reasonable solution can be sought by a third person.

要点概述

（2）其程序受法律规范约束少。在线调解中，可以通过第三人寻求一种合理的解决方法。

(3) The third person is a third person who is willing and has no interest. In the US Oline ADR investigation process, mediation is usually conducted by consumer associations, business associations or some neutral institutions.

要点概述

（3）第三人为自愿且无利害关系的第三人。美国 Oline ADR 的调查程序中，通常是由消费者协会、商业协会或一些中立机构来进行调解。

10.3 Talent cultivation

10.3.1 Introduction

The rapid development of cross-border e-commerce has provided a huge demand for talents in this field. China's e-commerce transaction volume in 2015 was 18.3 trillion yuan. According to a survey by the China Electronic Commerce Research Center, in 2015, 85.9% of companies believe that there is a serious gap in cross-border e-commerce business. With the support of the "Internet +" national policy, more traditional enterprises borrow cross-border e-commerce to expand the market, promote industrial upgrading, and meet the needs of cross-border e-commerce talent. The completion of the entire trading activity involves not only information flow, fund types, physical distribution on a global scale, but also the exchange of legal, economic and cultural fields in different countries or regions. According to a survey, the talents of existing companies choosing cross-border power suppliers are more inclined to international trade professionals, followed by e-commerce professionals, and 65.1% of respondents urgently need compound talents.

要点概述

跨境电子商务的快速发展为该领域提供了一个巨大的人才需求。2015 年中国电子商务交易额 18.3 万亿元。根据中国电子商务研究中心的调查，在 2015 年，85.9% 的公司认为跨境电子商务的业务存在严重的差距。在“互联网+”的国家政策支持下，更传统的企业借用跨境电子商务来扩大市场，促进产业升级，满足跨境电子商务人才的需求。整个交易活动的完成不仅仅涉及信息流、基金类别、全球范围内的实物分销，同时涉及不同的国家或地区在法律、经济、文化领域的交流。一项调查显示，现有企业选择跨境电子商务人才更倾向于国际贸易专业人士，其次是电子商务专业人士，65.1% 的受访企业表示迫切需要复合型人才。

Cross-border e-commerce trade in the rapid development, and gradually exposed the comprehensive foreign trade talent gap serious problems.

The main reason for the lack of cross-border electricity merchants is because:

要点概述

跨境电子商务贸易在快速发展的同时，也逐渐暴露出复合型外贸人才缺口大的问题。

跨境电商人才缺失主要是因为：

(1) Language restriction: At present, the talents who do cross-border e-commerce mainly come from the foreign trade industry, but there are many English majors, and some small-language electric merchants are lacking. But in fact, in Brazil, India, Russia, Arabia, Mongolia and other countries, cross-border e-commerce has great potential for development and is also the focus of cross-border e-commerce companies.

要点概述

（1）语种限制。目前做跨境电商的人才主要还是来自外贸行业，但英语专业居多，一些小语种电商人才缺乏，但事实上，像巴西、印度、俄罗斯、阿拉伯、蒙古等国家，跨境电商具有很大的发展潜力，也是跨境电商企业关注的重点。

(2) High ability requirements: In addition to the restrictions of language, talents engaged in cross-border e-commerce business must also be able to understand foreign markets, trading methods, consumption habits, etc. In addition, they must understand the trading rules and transaction features of major platforms.

要点概述

（2）能力要求高。从事跨境电商业务的人才，除了语种的限制外，还要能了解国外的市场、交易方式、消费习惯等，此外，还要了解各大平台的交易规则和交易特征。

Based on these two characteristics, there are few talents who meet the requirements of cross-border e-commerce. The lack of cross-border electricity merchants has become the norm in the industry.

要点概述

基于这两个特点，满足跨境电子商务需求的人才寥寥无几。跨境电商的缺失已成为行业的常态。

10.3.2 Training cross-border e-commerce talents

The government should guide the direction of the cross-border e-commerce talents training, on-site support for cross-border e-commerce talents training and financial support, and improve the transnational e-commerce personnel qualification system, create a good talent policy and company policy to encourage cross-border e-commerce talents training of enterprise, and promote enterprise and in colleges and universities to establish the relationship between the order type training and cooperation mechanism.

要点概述

政府应该引导跨境电子商务人才培养的方向，跨境电子商务人才培养提供现场支持和金融支持，提高跨境电子商务人才资格制度，创造良好的人才政策和公司政策鼓励地区跨境电子商务企业参与人才培养，并促进企业和高校建立订单式培训和合作机制之间的关系。

Government should be encouraged to third party training institutions for cross-border e-commerce related business training, the university graduates through fiscal subsidy way, accept the third-party training institutions to carry out the business of pre-service training, shorten the work period of fresh graduates, encourage cross-border e-commerce enterprise business promotion personnel training, to strengthen cross-border e-commerce talents reserve capacity of the enterprise.

要点概述

鼓励第三方培训机构开展跨境电子商务相关业务培训，对大学毕业生通过财政补贴方式，接受第三方培训机构开展业务的岗前培训，缩短应届毕业生的工作周期，鼓励跨境电子商务企业加强人员培训，加强跨境电子商务企业的人才储备能力。

Notes:

1. Customs formality

海关是负责征收关税和控制是流通包括动物、运输、个人和危险物品等进出一个国家的国家的权威机构，是依据本国（或地区）的法律、行政法规行使进出口监督管理职权的国家行政机关。英语 Customs 一词，最早是指商人贩运商品途中缴纳的一种地方税捐，带有“买路钱”或港口、市场“通过费”“使用费”的性质。这种地方税捐取消后，Customs 一词则专指政府征收的进出口税，the Customs 是征收进出口税的政府机构，即海关，是对出入国境的一切商品和物品进行监督、检查并照章征收关税的国家机关。

2. ODR

在线纠纷解决机制（ODR）是利用网络技术来促进解决当事人之间的争端的一种机制，主要涉及谈判、调解或仲裁或者三者的结合。ODR 通常认为是从替代性纠纷解决机制（ADR）演化而来的。

3. K9

K9 特指警犬和军犬，是根据犬的英文单词 Canine 的谐音而得来，这个编号深受官方和公众的欢迎，很快就风靡开来。在美国，一些警犬部门和培训基地都采用 K9 这个称呼。

Review questions:

According to the topic of this chapter, briefly answer the following questions:

(1) What is the definition and method of online dispute resolution mechanism

(2) What are the customs issues in cross-border e-commerce?

(3) How should the government strengthen the training of talents?

Chapter 11

Prospect of Cross-border E-commerce

The four major challenges facing cross-border e-commerce: The first is capacity building. Digital transformation is the transformation of everyone and every enterprise. Continuous iterative innovation of technology and business models, and even subversive developments, have placed high demands on the understanding and capabilities of business managers and employees. The second is infrastructure. Now the target market for cross-border e-commerce is expanding from developed countries in Europe and America to more developing countries, and local logistics and payment systems, including imperfections in the Internet and telecommunications infrastructure, will create obstacles and bottlenecks to the expansion of e-commerce companies. The third is that policy changes will bring confusion and impact to enterprises. Many countries are now preparing to adjust cross-border e-commerce policies, including some important markets such as Russia, the European Union, Australia, etc. We must actively pay attention to the development of these national policies. The fourth is market competition. At present, the phenomenon of cross-border e-commerce homogenization competition is more obvious. More and more companies are engaged in the cross-border e-commerce industry. Our company must focus on consumers, through data accumulation and analysis, work hard to improve the international competitiveness of products, services and enterprises, and strive to increase the added value of products, including in the product differentiation, personalization, internationalization and branding to find directions. At the same time, we must pay attention to protecting intellectual property rights.

要点概述

跨境电商面临的四大挑战：第一是能力建设。数字化转型是对每个人、每个企业的转型。技术和商业模式的不断迭代创新，甚至颠覆性的发展变化，都对企业管理者和员工的认识和能力，提出了较高的要求。第二是基础设施。现在跨境电商的目标市场正在从欧美发达国家扩大到更多的发展中国家，而当地物流、支付体系，包括互联网和电信基础设施的不完善，都会对电商企业的业务拓展形成障碍和瓶颈。第三是政策变化会给企业带来困惑和影响。现在很多国家都在准备调整跨境电商政策，包括一些重要市场如俄罗斯、欧盟、澳大利亚等，我们要积极关注这些国家政策的发展变化。第四是市场竞争。目前，跨境电商同质化竞争现象比较明显。随着越来越多的企业从事跨境电商，我们的企业一定要以消费者为核心，通过数据积累和分析，在提升产品、服务和企业自身的国际竞争力下功夫，努力增加产品附加值，包括在产品的“差异化、个性化、国际化、品牌化”几个方面找方向，同时一定要注重保护好知识产权。

11.1 The trend of economic development under the new situation

In recent years, network technology has developed rapidly, and a large number of traditional foreign trade enterprises have used the network to open up the international market in order to switch to the e-commerce market more efficiently and at low cost. Cross-border e-commerce companies have developed vigorously with cross-border micro-transactions, replacing the long-single mode of the original large and medium-sized wholesalers. In contrast, domestic e-commerce has matured over the years. Many companies and individuals have entered e-commerce, and competition has become increasingly fierce. Profit margins have become lower and lower with the increase in the cost of talent, logistics, and advertising.

要点概述

近年来，网络技术发展迅速，大批的传统外贸企业为了更高效、低成本转战电商市场，利用网络开辟国际市场。跨境电商企业以跨境小额交易为主蓬勃发展起来，代替了原有大中型批发商的长单模式。相比之下，中国的电子商务经过这些年的发展已经非常成熟，很多企业和个人进入电子商务，竞争日趋激烈，利润率随着人才、物流、广告等成本的提高，越来越低。

The four driving forces for the development of china’s cross-border e-commerce industry:

要点概述

中国跨境电商发展的四大驱动力：

(1) Technological innovation. Without the Internet, mobile Internet and intelligent terminals, there could be no development of e-commerce and cross-border electric business. We hope that our countries and enterprises can attach great importance to the development and application of new technologies, including large data, cloud computing, Internet of things and artificial intelligence, and consider the future business infrastructure to be perfected. This will be the basic condition for China's digital economy and cross-border e-commerce to continue to develop and lead the world.

要点概述

（1）技术创新。假如没有互联网、移动互联网和智能终端等，就不可能有电子商务和跨境电商的发展。希望我们的国家和企业，能够高度重视包括大数据、云计算、物联网、人工智能等新技术的发展和应用，并视为未来商业的基础设施去完善。这将是中国数字经济和跨境电商能够持续发展和领跑全球的基础条件。

(2) China's huge market. The number of Chinese online shoppers has reached 500 million last year, and the figure is increasing. But compared with developed countries, China's Internet users are not a high proportion of cross-border online purchases, there is still much room for development and growth potential in the future. We expect that the future cross-border electric business related Chinese net-purchase user share and sales will continue to grow faster. China's middle class is also growing, with 200 million middle-class households expected by 2020. A huge market can attract overseas exports to China, and it will also help to strengthen China's voice and influence in the world.

要点概述

（2）中国巨大的市场。去年中国网购用户已经达到5亿人，而且这个数字还在增加。但是与发达国家相比，中国互联网用户的跨境网购比例并不算高，未来还有很大的发展空间和增长潜力。我们预计，未来跨境电商相关的中国网购用户占比和销售额还将继续较快增长。中国中产阶级也在不断增加，预计到2020年中国中产阶级会达到2亿户。一个巨大的市场能够吸引海外对中国的出口，也有助于增强中国在全球的话语权和影响力。

(3) China is the world's factory. China is turning from a manufacturing powerhouse to a manufacturing powerhouse, and tens of millions of China's small and medium-sized

enterprises have played a very important role in China's manufacturing development and foreign trade. Excellent manufacturing enterprises, production technology, skilled workers, a wide range of industrial system, for the development of China's cross-border electric power provider provides a very good foundation condition. We sell China's quality products through cross-border electric dealers, and at the same time drive the transformation and upgrading of related services.

要点概述

（3）中国是世界工厂。中国正在从制造大国变成制造强国，中国几千万的中小微企业为中国制造业发展和对外贸易发挥了非常重要的作用。优秀的制造企业、生产技术、熟练工人、门类齐全的工业体系，为中国发展跨境电商提供了一个非常好的基础条件。我们通过跨境电商把中国优质的产品卖出去，同时可以驱动相关服务业的转型升级。

(4) Credit Guarantee. Two people who don't know each other conduct trade activities. Without a trust mechanism, transactions are impossible. With the development of third-party payment platforms such as Alipay and the continuous improvement of China's online transaction credit system, including the personal credit established by social networking, human beings are slowly establishing a global network enterprise and personal credit mechanism. This is also an important basis for the healthy development of cross-border e-commerce.

要点概述

（4）信用保障。我们知道，两个不认识的人做贸易，如果没有一种信任机制，交易是不可能达成的。随着支付宝等第三方支付平台的发展，以及中国网络交易信用体系的不断完善，包括网络社交建立起来的个人信用，人类正在慢慢建立一个覆盖全球的网络企业和个人信用机制。这也是跨境电商能够健康发展的一个重要基础。

11.2 More profits in the foreign trade market

The foreign trade market has more lucrative profits. Foreign trade is facing a broader international market, and it is a brand new market development for new markets and potential markets. Cross-border e-commerce can directly face foreign consumers, reduce the loss of intermediate links, have more lucrative profits, and will become a new international trade model. If you can make good use of this opportunity, you can get more benefits than domestic trade e-commerce.

要点概述

外贸市场具有更为丰厚的利润。外贸面对的是更为广阔的国际市场，对新市场及潜在市场来说，是一个全新的市场开发。跨境电子商务能够直接面对国外消费者，减少了中间环节损失，具有更加丰厚的利润，将成为一个新的国际贸易模式，如果能够很好地利用这个机会，可以得到比内贸电子商务更多的效益。

Through the cross-border e-commerce model, SMEs can reduce costs in various aspects such as publicity, logistics, customs clearance, etc., and invest the saved funds in technology research and development and quality improvement, and create competitive self-owned brands by improving research and development capabilities, then enter the international market with the help of cross-border e-commerce platforms. For some large-scale state-owned enterprises, they can also enhance their visibility and comprehensive strength in the international market by leveraging the convenience advantages of cross-border e-commerce and foreign trade.

要点概述

通过跨境电商模式，中小企业可以在宣传、物流、通关等多个方面减少成本，并将节省出来的资金投入到技术研发及质量提升等层面，通过提高研发能力打造具有竞争力的自有品牌，再借助跨境电商平台打入国际市场。对于一些规模较大的国有企业而言，同样可以借助跨境电商与国外贸易的便利优势，提升自己在国际市场的知名度及综合实力。

Challenges for cross-border e-commerce:

The first is capacity building. Digital transformation is the transformation of everyone and every enterprise. Continuous iterative innovation of technology and business models, and even subversive developments, have placed high demands on the understanding and capabilities of business managers and employees. The second is infrastructure. Now the target market for cross-border e-commerce is expanding from developed countries in Europe and America to more developing countries, and local logistics and payment systems, including imperfections in the Internet and telecommunications infrastructure, will create obstacles and bottlenecks to the expansion of e-commerce companies. The third is that policy changes will bring confusion and impact to enterprises. Many countries are now preparing to adjust cross-border e-commerce policies, including some important markets such as Russia, the European Union, Australia, etc. We must actively pay attention to the development of these national policies. At the same time, we must actively guide and optimize the policy direction through the study of "official industry and industry" and international exchanges and cooperation. The fourth is market competition. At present, the phenomenon of cross-border e-commerce homogenization competition is more obvious. As more and more companies engage in cross-border e-commerce, our company must focus on consumers, through data accumulation and analysis, work hard to improve the international competitiveness of products, services and enterprises, and strive to increase product add-on values, including the direction of "differentiation, personalization, internationalization, branding" of products.We must also focus on protecting intellectual property rights.

要点概述

跨境电商面临的挑战：

第一是能力建设。数字化转型是对每个人、每个企业的转型。技术和商业模式的不断迭代创新，甚至颠覆性的发展变化，都对企业管理者和员工的认识和能力，提出了较高的要求。第二是基础设施。现在跨境电商的目标市场，正在从欧美发达国家扩大到更多的发展中国家，而当地物流、支付体系，包括互联网和电信基础设施的不完善，都会对电商企业的业务拓展形成障碍和瓶颈。第三是政策变化会给企业带来困惑和影响。现在很多国家都在准备调整跨境电商政策，包括一些重要市场如俄罗斯、欧盟、澳大利亚等，我们要积极关注这些国家政策的发展变化。同时，我们还要积极通过"官产学"研究和国际交流合作，去引导和优化政策走向。第四是市场竞争。目前，跨境电商同质化竞争现象比较明显。随着越来越多的企业从事跨境电商，我们的企业一定要以消费者为核心，通过数据积累和分析，在提升产品、服务和企业自身的国际竞争力下功夫，努力增加产品附加值，包括在产品的"差异化、个性化、国际化、品牌化"找方向，同时一定要注重保护好知识产权。

11.3 Great space for development

B2B e-commerce accounts for 83.5% of the turnover in the domestic e-commerce market, according to a market research report from the cross-border electricity industry. However, B2B e-commerce cannot be used to complete on-line transactions, its actual profit space compared to the online shopping power is very small. This is also the main reason why there are no big B2B e-commerce companies in the world compared to online shopping companies such as Taobao and Amazon. Therefore, the development space for realizing B2B online transactions by using cross-border e-commerce is still very large.

要点概述

跨境电商行业市场研究报告显示，当前，中国 B2B 电商占了国内电商市场交易额的 83.5%。但商对商电子商务无法完成网上交易，其实际盈利空间相比网上购物电商小很多，这也是相比淘宝、亚马逊等在线网上购物公司，全球都没有产生特别大的 B2B 电子商务公司的主要原因。因此，利用跨境电商来实现 B2B 在线交易的发展空间还是很大的。

In the future, the B2B model will more reflect the characteristics of cross-border electric power, through the manufacturing enterprises to promote B2B cross-border electricity, better promote the integration of foreign trade services enterprises and modern logistics enterprises transformation. The B2C model will usher in a period of rapid growth, and the integration of traffic resources across platforms may be the future trend.

要点概述

今后 B2B 模式将更多体现跨境电商特点，通过制造业企业推动 B2B 跨境电商，更好促进外贸综合服务企业和现代物流企业的转型。B2C 模式将迎来快速增长时期，B2C 跨平台整合流量资源或许将是未来发展趋势。

First, future B2B will evolve from an information platform to a trading platform. Alibaba's B2B platform is developing into a closed-loop, full link, full-featured eco-platform. Only by forming a closed loop of transactions and services, through the precipitation and analysis of platform data, can we provide better and more services for small and medium-sized enterprises on the platform, including customs clearance, trade financing, credit guarantee, logistics arrangements, digital marketing, exchange of funds and tax refund, etc. Second, B2C will become one of the two major forms of trade in international trade. Especially with the development of cross-border e-commerce, many traders who used to be in the middle of the chain will gradually become service providers. Third, the service ecology will be more prosperous. Whether it is financial payment, logistics and warehousing, including the current popular overseas warehouses, digital marketing, intellectual property protection, and electric merchant training, it will develop in the direction of specialization, synergy and internationalization, and play an important role in the e-commerce service system. Fourth, cross-border e-commerce will promote the development of new international trade rules and standards.

要点概述

第一，未来 B2B 会从信息平台发展成为一个交易平台。阿里巴巴的 B2B 平台正在向一个闭环的、全链路、功能齐全的生态平台发展。只有形成交易和服务的闭环，通过平台数据的沉淀和分析，才能为平台上的中小微企业提供更好更多的服务，包括报关通关、贸易融资、信用担保、物流安排、数字营销、换汇退税等。第二，B2C会成为国际贸易的两大贸易形式之一。尤其是随着跨境电商的发展，很多过去处于中间环节的贸易商，会逐渐转变为服务商。第三，服务生态会更加繁荣。无论是金融支付、物流仓储，包括现在流行的海外仓，还是数字营销、知识产权保护、电商人才培养，都会朝专业化、协同化和国际化的方向发展，在电子商务服务体系中发挥重要作用。第四，跨境电商会推动新的国际贸易规则和标准的发展。

Notes:

产官学

产官学结合 (the Combination of Industry, Official and University) 中的“产”是指产业界、企业，“官”是指政府，“学”是指学术界，包括大学与科研机构等。

Review questions:

According to the topic of this chapter, briefly answer the following questions:

(1) What is the prospect of Cross-border e-business?

(2) What is the development of foreign trade market?

Glossary

社交电子商务 Social commerce	Social e-commerce is based on the network of interpersonal relationships. The use of Internet social tools to engage in the sales of goods or services is one of the important manifestations of new e-commerce. It uses social networking sites, SNS, Weibo, social media, and online media to assist in the purchase and sale of goods through social interactions and user-generated content. 社交电子商务是基于人际关系网络，利用互联网社交工具，从事商品或服务销售的经营行为，是新型电子商务的重要表现形式之一。它借助社交网站、SNS、微博、社交媒介、网络媒介的传播途径，通过社交互动、用户自生内容等手段来辅助商品的购买和销售行为。
B2Q 模式 The B2Q model (introduction of quality control by enterprise online shopping)	The B2Q model (introduction of quality control by enterprise online shopping) is essentially based on the B2B and B2C models, and creatively introduces an innovative model of quality control, which is an innovation that responds to market demands. In the B2Q mode, both parties to the transaction first reach an intent transaction contract. After signing the order, they can enter the third-party (inspection, inspection, equipment commissioning) engineers to conduct commodity quality inspection and after-sale installation and commissioning services according to the buyer's needs. B2Q 模式（企业网购引入质量控制），从本质来讲是建立在 B2B 和 B2C 模式的基础上，创造性地引入了质量控制的创新模式，是一种应对市场需求的创新。B2Q 模式的交易双方网上先达成意向交易合同，签单后根据买方需要可引进入第三方（验货、验厂、设备调试）工程师进行商品品质检验及售后安装调试服务。
厂商到消费者模式 F2C	F2C refers to Factory to customer, that is, the e-commerce model from the manufacturer to the consumer: the brand company delivers the designed product to the consumer through the terminal after the factory is found, ensuring that the product is reasonable and the quality service is guaranteed. They provide consumers with a cost-effective product. F2C（Factory to customer），即从厂商到消费者的电子商务模式：品牌公司把设计好的产品交由工厂代工后通过终端送达消费者，同时质量服务都有保证。它们为消费者提供了性价比高的产品。

续表

个性化营销 Personalized marketing	Personalized marketing means that the company pushes the attention of people, the release of people' s personality and the needs of people's individuality to an unprecedented center, establishes a personal database and information files for consumers, establishes a more personal connection with consumers, learns about market trends and real customer needs, and provides customers with a personalized sales and service. Data collection methods, analysis, and advances in the digital economy have made it possible for companies to provide customers with more timely, effective, and personalized marketing methods. 个性化营销即企业把对人的关注、人的个性释放及人的个性需求的满足推到空前中心的地位，建立消费者个人数据库和信息档案，与消费者建立更为个人化的联系，及时地了解市场动向和顾客真正需求，向顾客提供一种个人化的销售和服务。数据收集方式、分析和数字经济的进步，使得企业为顾客提供更及时有效、更个性化的营销方式成为可能。
ERP 系统 Enterprise resource planning	ERP system is the abbreviation of Enterprise Resource Planning. It refers to a management platform for decision-making means for employees with a systematic management idea. It can comprehensively manage the core business processes based on the establishment of information technology, through the timely deployment of software and technology, with the combination of information technology and advanced management ideas. It typically includes a comprehensive set of business management software that collects, stores, manages, and interprets data collected from business activities. ERP 系统 (Enterprise Resource Planning，企业资源计划），是指建立在信息技术基础上，通过软件和科技的及时调配，对核心商业流程进行综合性管理，集信息技术与先进管理思想于一身，以系统化的管理思想，为企业员工及决策层提供决策手段的管理平台。它通常包含一整套综合性的商业管理软件，能够收集、储存、管理、解释从商业活动中收集到的数据。
电子商务支付系统 E-commerce payment system	An e-commerce payment system refers to the exchange of goods or services between consumers, businesses and financial institutions using secure electronic means. That is, the payment means of the new payment means, including electronic cash, credit card, debit card, smart card, etc., are securely transmitted to the bank or the corresponding processing institution through the network to realize electronic payment. It is a comprehensive system integrating shopping processes, payment tools, security technology, certification system, credit system and modern financial system. 电子商务支付系统是指消费者、商家和金融机构之间使用安全电子手段交换商品或服务，即把新型支付手段包括电子现金、信用卡、借记卡、智能卡等支付信息通过网络安全传送到银行或相应的处理机构来实现电子支付，是融购物流程、支付工具、安全技术、认证体系、信用体系以及现代的金融体系为一体的综合大系统。

续表

团购 Group purchase	Group purchase is a kind of shopping method in which consumers who know or don't know each other together to increase their bargaining chips with merchants and get the best price, according to the principle of small profit and excessive sales. Businesses can offer group buying discounts below retail prices and quality services that cannot be obtained by individual purchases. 团购就是团体线上购物，指认识或不认识的消费者联合起来，加大与商家的谈判筹码，会取得最优价格的一种购物方式。根据薄利多销的原则，商家可以给出低于零售价格的团购折扣和单独购买得不到的优质服务。
付费点击 PPC	Pay Per Click (PPC), also known as Cost per Click (CPC), is an internet advertising model used to direct traffic to websites, in which an advertiser pays a publisher (typically a website owner or a network of websites) when the ad is clicked. With search engines, advertisers typically bid on keyword phrases relevant to their target market. In contrast, content sites commonly charge a fixed price per click rather than use a bidding system. 付费点击（Pay Per Click）也称作 Cost Per Click（CPC），是一种网络广告的收费计算形式，广泛用在搜寻引擎、广告网络、以及网站或博客等网络广告平台。规则是只有当使用者实际上点击广告以拜访广告主的网站时，广告主才需要支付费用。广告主可以竞标他们认定的目标市场对象在寻找某一种类的产品或者服务时，在搜寻时可能会输入的关键字。
网络外部性 network externality	Network externality is an important concept in the new economy, meaning that the value of connecting to a network depends on the number of other people connected to the network. In layman’s terms, the utility that each user gets from using a product is positively related to the total number of users. The greater the number of users, the higher the utility each user gets, and the value of everyone in the network is proportional to the number of other people on the network. This also means that the increase in the number of network users will drive the geometric progression of the total user utility. 网络外部性是新经济中的重要概念，是指连接到一个网络的价值取决于已经连接到该网络的其他人的数量。通俗地说，就是每个用户从使用某产品中得到的效用与用户的总数量正相关。用户人数越多，每个用户得到的效用就越高，网络中每个人的价值与网络中其他人的数量成正比。这也就意味着网络用户数量的增长，将会带动用户总所得效用的几何级数增长。
《2002 年电子商务 (EC Directive) 规例》 *Electronic Commerce Regulations 2002*	*The Electronic Commerce (EC Directive) Regulations 2002*, incorporates the EU Electronic Commerce Directive 2000/31/EC into the law of the United Kingdom. They apply to contracts concluded by electronic means over distance whereby the buyer is a consumer. This subordinate legislation provides for rights of the consumer and provisions for which the seller is obliged to fulfill. 《2002 年电子商务 (EC Directive) 规例》将欧盟电子商务指令 2000/31/EC 纳入英国法律。它们适用于以电子方式结束的合同，即买方是消费者。这一附属法例规定了消费者的权利和卖方必须履行的规定。

续表

双边市场 Two-sided markets	Two-sided markets, also called two-sided networks, are economic platforms having two distinct user groups that provide each other with network benefits. The organization that creates value primarily by enabling direct interactions between two (or more) distinct types of affiliated customers is called a multi-sided platform (MSP). 双边市场，也被称为双边网络，是有两个互相提供网络收益的独立用户群体的经济网络。这个定义只是从普及概念的角度给出了一个描述性的介绍，而对经济研究而言还不够严谨。双边（更一般的说是多边）市场是一个或几个允许最终用户交易的平台，通过适当的从各方收取费用使双边（或多边）保留在平台上。
移动电子商务 Mobile commerce	Mobile commerce is B2B, B2C, C2C or O2O e-commerce carried out by wireless terminals such as mobile phones and PDA. It is the perfect union of the Internet, mobile communication technology, short distance communication technology and other information processing technology, which enables people to conduct various business activities at any time and any place, realizing anytime, anywhere, online and offline shopping and trading, online electronic payment and various trading activities, business activities, financial activities and related comprehensive service activities. 移动电子商务就是利用手机、PDA 及掌上电脑等无线终端进行的 B2B、B2C、C2C 或 O2O 的电子商务。它将因特网、移动通信技术、短距离通信技术及其他信息处理技术完美的结合，使人们可以在任何时间、任何地点进行各种商贸活动，实现随时随地、线上线下的购物与交易、在线电子支付以及各种交易活动、商务活动、金融活动和相关的综合服务活动等。
移动票务 Mobile ticketing	Mobile ticketing is the process whereby customers can order, pay for, obtain and validate tickets using mobile phones or other mobile handsets. Mobile tickets reduce the production and distribution costs connected with traditional paper-based ticketing channels and increase customer convenience by providing new and simple ways to purchase tickets. In terms of safety, paper tickets are easily lost and damaged, and there is no such problem with electronic tickets purchased through the mobile ticketing system. 移动票务是指顾客使用移动电话或其他移动设备订购、支付、取票和检验票券的过程，它代表了一个日益扩大的新兴市场。移动票务与传统购票相比的确有较强的优势。首先，与传统纸质门票相比，移动门票省时省力；其次，在安全性方面，纸票容易丢失、损坏，通过移动票务系统购买的电子票则不存在这样的问题。
移动电商服务提供商 Mobile commerce service provider	A mobile commerce service provider (mCSP) is an organization (or company) that provides any combination of consulting, software and computer systems for mobile e-commerce platforms, mobile devices (cellular phones, smart phones), mobile commerce, mobile content or mobile web sites. mCSP 是一个组织（或公司），为移动电子商务平台、移动设备（手机、智能手机）、移动商务、移动内容或移动 web 站点提供咨询、软件和计算机系统的任何组合。

续表

网络经济 Network economy	The network economy is a new economic form based on computer networks (especially the Internet) and modern information technology. It not only refers to the rise and rapid growth of the computer-based information technology industry, but also the rise and rapid development of the entire high-tech industry based on modern computer technology, including the profound revolutionary changes and rapid development the tradition industrial and traditional economic sectors caused by the promotion and application of high-tech. 网络经济，一种建立在计算机网络 (特别是 Internet) 基础之上，以现代信息技术为核心的新的经济形态。它不仅是指以计算机为核心的信息技术产业的兴起和快速增长，也包括以现代计算机技术为基础的整个高新技术产业的崛起和迅猛发展，更包括由于高新技术的推广和运用所引起的传统产业、传统经济部门的深刻的革命性变化和飞跃性发展。
增值网 Value Added Network	Value-added network refers to an information system that exchanges information of related departments such as manufacturing, wholesale, retail, and logistics industries through computer service networks. The value-added network can use the transmission equipment leased from the public network, and use the department's switches, computers and other special equipment to form a private network to meet the needs of the department. Examples include a fax storage and forwarding network composed of a high-speed channel, a conference television network, a private packet switching network, a virtual private network (VPN), and the like. 增值网是指将制造业、批发业、零售业、物流业等相关部门的信息，通过计算机服务网络来相互交换的信息系统。增值网可凭借从公用网租用的传输设备，使用本部门的交换机、计算机和其它专用设备组成专用网，以适应本部门的需要。例如，租用高速信道组成的传真存储转发网、会议电视网、专用分组交换网、虚拟专用网（VPN）等。
软件运营 Software as a service	Software as a service(SaaS) is an application model based on the Internet to provide software services. With the development of Internet technology and the maturity of application software, SaaS has emerged as an innovative software application model. Soft company provides all the network infrastructure and software and hardware operation platforms needed for informationization, and is responsible for all the services such as pre-implementation and post-operation maintenance. Enterprises can use information systems via the Internet without purchasing hardware and software, building computer rooms, and hiring IT staff. Just like opening a tap to use water, companies can rent software services to soft companies based on actual needs. 软件运营是一种基于互联网提供软件服务的应用模式。随着互联网技术的发展和应用软件的成熟，SaaS 作为一种创新的软件应用模式逐渐兴起。软营公司为企业搭建信息化所需的所有网络基础设施及软硬件运作平台，并负责所有前期实施、后期运营维护等一系列服务，企业无须购买软硬件、建设机房、招聘 IT 人员，即可通过互联网使用信息系统。就像打开自来水龙头就能用水一样，企业根据实际需要，向软营公司租赁软件服务。

续表

直销方式 direct selling	The direct sales method is an efficient marketing method that removes the middlemen, reduces the cost of the circulation of the product, and satisfies the needs of the customer. In short, it is a sales model in which the manufacturer does not go through the middlemen but sells the goods directly to the customer, reducing the intermediate links and the cost of sales. In the non-direct sales mode, there are two sales teams, the first is the manufacturer selling to the dealer, and the second is the dealer selling to the customer. 直销方式就是通过去掉中间商，降低产品的流通环节成本并满足顾客利益最大化需求的一种效率高的营销方式。简言之，就是生产商不经过中间商直接把商品销售到顾客手中的、减少中间环节和销售成本的一种销售模式。在非直销方式中，有两支销售队伍，第一条是制造商销售给经销商，第二条是经销商销售给顾客。
4Ps 理论 The 4Ps marketing theory	The 4Ps marketing theory is a foundation model in marketing. The marketing mix has been defined as the "set of marketing tools that the firm uses to pursue its marketing objectives in the target". Thus the marketing mix refers to four broad levels of marketing decision, namely: product, price, promotion, and place. 4P 营销理论是市场营销的基本模式，被归结为四个基本策略的组合，即产品（product）、价格（price）、渠道（place）、宣传（promotion），由于这四个词的英文字头都是 P，再加上策略（strategy），所以简称为"4Ps"
4C 营销理论 The 4C marketing theory	The 4C marketing theory was proposed in 1990 by the American marketing expert professor Lauter Peng. Corresponding to the 4P of traditional marketing, it resets the four basic elements of the marketing mix, namely consumer, cost, convenience and communication, based on Consumer demand. 4C 营销理论，是由美国营销专家劳特朋教授在 1990 年提出的，与传统营销的 4P 相对应。它以消费者需求为导向，重新设定了市场营销组合的四个基本要素：即消费者（consumer）、成本（cost）、便利（convenience）和沟通（communication）。
敦煌网 DHgate.com	DHgate.com is the world's leading online foreign trade trading platform. It is the first website in China to provide B2B online transactions for SMEs. It adopts a commission system, which is free of registration fees and is charged only after the transaction between the buyer and the seller is successful. It also provides international payment services, logistics services, custody protection services and internet financial services. 敦煌网是全球领先的在线外贸交易平台。敦煌网是国内首个为中小企业提供 B2B 网上交易的网站。它采取佣金制，免注册费，只在买卖双方交易成功后收取费用。它还提供国际支付服务、物流服务、托管保护服务和互联网金融服务。

续表

海淘 Overseas online shopping	Haitao is overseas/overseas shopping, which is to retrieve overseas product information through the Internet, and send a shopping request through an electronic order form, and then fill in a private credit card number. The commodity is delivered by an overseas shopping website through international express delivery, or by a transshipment company, then it is sent to the country. It is divided into two types: domestic cross-border e-commerce purchasing and overseas direct mail direct purchase. The rise of "Hao Tao" has benefited from the increasingly convenient online shopping channels, and the increase in the purchasing power of domestic consumers and the enhancement of the international payment ability of the RMB are also important reasons. 海淘即海外 / 境外购物，就是通过互联网检索海外商品信息，并通过电子订购单发出购物请求，然后填上私人信用卡号码，由海外购物网站通过国际快递发货，或是由转运公司代收货物再转寄回国。境外购物分为国内跨境电商代购和海外直邮直购两类。“海淘”的兴起得益于日益便捷的网络购物渠道，而国内消费者购买力的提高以及人民币国际支付能力的增强也是重要原因。
美国联邦快递 FedEx	FedEx is the world's largest express delivery company, providing fast and reliable courier services to more than 220 countries and regions around the world, providing customers with a comprehensive range of services covering transportation, e-commerce and business operations. 联邦快递是全球最具规模的快递运输公司，为全球超过 220 个国家及地区提供快捷、可靠的快递服务，为客户提供涵盖运输、电子商务和商业运作等一系列的全面服务。
UPS 快递 United Parcel Service	Founded in 1907 as a messenger company in Seattle, Washington, USA, United Parcel Service is a global company whose trademark is one of the world's leading trademarks. As the world's largest express carrier and package delivery company, it is also a leading provider of transportation, logistics, capital and e-commerce services. UPS 快递 (United Parcel Service) 在 1907 年作为一家信使公司成立于美国华盛顿州西雅图，是一家全球性的公司，其商标是世界上知名商标之一。作为世界上最大的快递承运商与包裹递送公司，同时也是运输、物流、资本与电子商务服务的领导性的提供者。
马士基 Maersk	Founded in 1904 and headquartered in Copenhagen, Denmark, Maersk Group has offices in 135 countries and employs approximately 89,000 people. It provides first-class service to its customers in container transportation, logistics, terminal operations, oil and gas exploration and production, and other activities related to the shipping and retail industries. Maersk Line, a subsidiary of Maersk Group, is the world' s largest container shipping company with a global service network. 马士基集团成立于 1904 年，总部位于丹麦哥本哈根，在全球 135 个国家设有办事机构，拥有约 89,000 名员工，在集装箱运输、物流、码头运营、石油和天然气开采与生产，以及与航运和零售行业相关其它活动中，为客户提供了一流的服务。马士基集团旗下的马士基航运是全球最大的集装箱承运公司，服务网络遍及全球。

续表

国际 e 邮宝 International E Post	International e post is a brand-new economical international postal product tailored by China Post to meet the needs of the international e-commerce delivery market. Like the Hong Kong International Parcel Service, International e post is an air-mail product for light and small items. Currently, this service is limited to parcel delivery services for Chinese e-commerce sellers to the US, Canada, UK, France and Australia. 国际 e 邮宝是中国邮政为适应国际电子商务寄递市场的需要，为中国电商卖家量身定制的一款全新经济型国际邮递产品。国际 e 邮宝和香港国际小包服务一样是针对轻小件物品的空邮产品，目前，该业务限于为中国电商卖家寄件人提供发向美国、加拿大、英国、法国和澳大利亚的包裹寄递服务。
保税区 Free economic zones	Free economic zones (FEZ), free economic territories (FETs) or free zones (FZ) are a class of special economic zone (SEZ) designated by the trade and commerce administrations of various countries. The term is used to designate areas in which companies are taxed very lightly or not at all to encourage economic activity. The taxation rules are determined by each country. The World Trade Organization (WTO) Agreement on Subsidies and Countervailing Measures (SCM) has content on the conditions and benefits of free zones. The bonded area, also known as the bonded warehouse area, is lower than the comprehensive bonded area. This is an area that can be stored for a longer period of time by a customs established by a country or approved by the customs and supervised and managed by the customs. It is an economic zone established by the State Council and implemented by the Customs for special supervision. 保税区，也称保税仓库区，级别低于综合保税区。这是一国海关设置的或经海关批准注册、受海关监督和管理的，可以较长时间存储商品的区域。是经国务院批准设立的、海关实施特殊监管的经济区域。
网络营销 Digital marketing	Digital marketing is the marketing of products or services using digital technologies, mainly on the Internet, but also including mobile phones, display advertising, and any other digital medium. Digital marketing's development since the 1990s and 2000s has changed the way brands and businesses use technology for marketing. As digital platforms are increasingly incorporated into marketing plans and everyday life, and as people use digital devices instead of visiting physical shops, digital marketing campaigns are becoming more prevalent and efficient. 网络营销是以现代营销理论为基础，借助网络、通信和数字媒体技术实现营销目标的商务活动，是科技进步、顾客价值变革、市场竞争等综合因素促成的，是信息化社会的必然产物。网络营销根据其实现方式有广义和狭义之分，广义的网络营销指企业利用一切计算机网络进行营销活动，而狭义的网络营销专指国际互联网营销。

续表

搜索引擎优化 Search Engine Optimization	Search Engine Optimization is a way to use search engine search rules to improve the current ranking of websites in search engines. The goal of SEO is to provide an ecological self-marketing solution for the website, allowing the website to take the lead in the industry and gain brand revenue. SEO includes both off-site SEO and on-site SEO. SEO refers to the behavior of making the website more suitable for the indexing principle of search engines in order to obtain more free traffic from the search engine, from the perspective of website structure, content construction plan, user interaction communication, and page. Search Engine Optimization（SEO）：汉译为搜索引擎优化。搜索引擎优化是一种利用搜索引擎的搜索规则来提高目前网站在有关搜索引擎内的自然排名的方式。SEO 的目的是：为网站提供生态式的自我营销解决方案，让网站在行业内占据领先地位，从而获得品牌收益；SEO 包含站外 SEO 和站内 SEO 两方面；SEO 是指为了从搜索引擎中获得更多的免费流量，从网站结构、内容建设方案、用户互动传播、页面等角度进行合理规划，使网站更适合搜索引擎的索引原则的行为。
EDM 营销 Email Direct Marketing	Email marketing is the act of sending a commercial message, typically to a group of people, using email. In its broadest sense, every email sent to a potential or current customer could be considered email marketing. It usually involves using email to send advertisements, request business, or solicit sales or donations, and is meant to build loyalty, trust, or brand awareness. EDM 营销也即：Email 营销、电子邮件营销。企业可以通过 EDM 建立同目标顾客的沟通渠道，向其直接传达相关信息，用来促进销售。EDM 有多种用途，可以发送电子广告、产品信息、销售信息、市场调查、市场推广活动信息等。
网络整合营销 Search engine marketing	Search engine marketing (SEM) is a form of Internet marketing that involves the promotion of websites by increasing their visibility in search engine results pages (SERPs) primarily through paid advertising. SEM may incorporate search engine optimization (SEO), which adjusts or rewrites website content and site architecture to achieve a higher ranking in search engine results pages to enhance pay per click (PPC) listings. SEM enables enterprises to use the new network marketing model to achieve real network marketing with the minimum investment, the shortest time, the most
网络整合营销 Search engine marketing	platforms and the maximum benefits, and constantly improve the visibility and brand exposure of enterprises, so that enterprise users can walk in the forefront of network marketing and become successful. SEM 是 Search Engine Marketing 的缩写，中文意思是搜索引擎营销或网络整合营销，是一种全新的互联网资源整合营销模式，整合了百度、谷歌、搜搜、搜狗等几大常用搜索引擎营销技术、知名主流综合性大型 B2B 平台阿里巴巴、赶集、58 同城、马可波罗等多家各行业知名网站优化技术以及视频、微博、博客、论坛、站群营销等网络营销推广手段，能更有效解决中小企业网络营销开展难、效果差、成本高、推广平台单一等瓶颈，今天 SEM 让企业利用新型的网络营销模式以最低投入、最短时间、最多平台、最大效益来实现真正的网络营销，不断提升企业知名度和品牌曝光率，让企业用户走在网络营销的前沿，走向成功。

续表

网络声誉管理 Online reputation management	The focus of online reputation management is the management of product and service search results within the digital space. Electronic markets and online communities such as e-Bay, Amazon, and Alibaba have established ORM systems that use effective control nodes to minimize threats and protect systems from misuse and abuse by malicious nodes in distributed overlay networks. 网络声誉管理的重点是在数字空间内对产品和服务搜索结果的管理。像e-Bay、亚马逊和阿里巴巴这样的电子市场和在线社区都建立了ORM系统，使用有效的控制节点可以最大限度地减少威胁，保护系统不受分散覆盖网络中恶意节点的误用和滥用。
信息不对称 Asymmetric information	Asymmetric information refers to the difference in information owned by each person in a transaction. In social, political, and economic activities, some members have information that other members cannot have, and thus information asymmetry caused. In the market economy activities, all kinds of personnel have different understandings of relevant information; those who have sufficient information are often in a relatively favorable position, while those with poor information are in a relatively disadvantageous position. Asymmetric information can lead to Adverse Selection. In general, sellers have more information about the transaction items than buyers, but counterexamples may exist. The former example can be seen in the sale and purchase of used cars, and the seller knows the sold vehicles more than the buyer. The latter example is medical insurance, and the buyer usually has more information. 信息不对称指交易中的各人拥有的信息不同。在社会政治、经济等活动中，一些成员拥有其他成员无法拥有的信息，由此造成信息的不对称。在市场经济活动中，各类人员对有关信息的了解是有差异的；掌握信息比较充分的人员，往往处于比较有利的地位，而信息贫乏的人员，则处于比较不利的地位。不对称信息可能导致逆向选择（Adverse Selection）。一般而言，卖家比买家拥有更多关于交易物品的信息，但反例也可能存在。前者例子可见于二手车的买卖，卖主对卖出的车辆比买方了解。后者例子如医疗保险，买方通常拥有更多信息。
网络安全 Network security	Network security means that the data in the hardware, software and systems of the network system is protected. It is not damaged, changed or leaked due to accidental or malicious reasons. The system runs continuously and reliably, and the network service is not interrupted. Network security includes policies and practices for preventing and monitoring unauthorized access, misuse, modification, or denial of computer network and network accessible resources. Network security involves the authorization of access to data in the network, which is controlled by the network administrator. The user selects or is assigned an ID and password or other authentication information that allows them to access information and programs within the permissions. 网络安全是指网络系统的硬件、软件及其系统中的数据受到保护，不因偶然的或者恶意的原因而遭受到破坏、更改、泄露，系统连续可靠正常地运行，网络服务不中断。网络安全包括用于预防和监控未经授权的访问、滥用、修改或拒绝计算机网络和网络可访问资源的政策和做法。网络安全涉及对网络中数据的访问授权，该网络由网络管理员控制。用户选择或被分配一个ID和密码或其他身份验证信息，允许他们访问权限内的信息和程序。

续表

网页设计 Web design	Web design is based on the information (including products, services, ideas, culture) that the company wants to deliver to the viewers, and then the website design and beautification work. As one of the company's external publicity materials, exquisite web design is essential to enhance the company's Internet brand image. Web design is generally divided into three major categories: functional web design (service website & B / S software client), image web design (brand image station), information web design (portal station). The purpose of designing a web page is different, and different webpage planning and design schemes should be selected. 网页设计是根据企业希望向浏览者传递的信息（包括产品、服务、理念、文化），进行网站功能策划，然后进行的页面设计美化工作。作为企业对外宣传物料的其中一种，精美的网页设计对于提升企业的互联网品牌形象至关重要。网页设计一般分为三类：功能型网页设计（服务网站 &B/S 软件用户端）、形象型网页设计（品牌形象站）、信息型网页设计（门户站）。设计网页的目的不同，应选择不同的网页策划与设计方案。
网络拍卖 Auction Online	Online auctions are a model of online transactions over the Internet. Online auction refers to the use of Internet communication transmission technology by network service providers to provide paid or free Internet technology platforms to commodity owners or certain rights holders. Online auctions allow commodity owners or certain equity owners to independently conduct bidding and bargaining-based online trading models on their platforms. 网络拍卖是通过因特网进行的在线交易的一种模式。网络拍卖指网络服务商利用互联网通信传输技术，向商品所有者或某些权益所有人提供有偿或无偿使用的互联网技术平台。网络拍卖让商品所有者或某些权益所有人在其平台上独立开展以竞价，议价方式为主的在线交易模式。
网络代理商 Network agent	A commercial organization or individual that uses the information transmission value of the network to achieve the purpose of selling products is called a network agent. Parallel to traditional channel vendors, sales methods and management methods are different from traditional channels. The core value of the network agent is: skilled and proficient in the use of network technology, the traditional offline sales program successfully transformed into a network sales program, to achieve multi-party cooperation, all-round win-win cooperation model. 利用网络的信息传输价值，实现销售产品目的的商业机构或个人，称为网络代理商。和传统的渠道商并列，销售手段和管理手段均有别于传统渠道。网络代理商的核心价值在于：熟练精通地运用网络的技术，将传统的线下销售方案成功地转化为网络销售方案，实现多方合作，全方位共赢的合作模式。

续表

安全电子交易协议 Secure Electronic Transaction	Secure Electronic Transaction (SET) is created by VISA International and MasterCard International, and is an international standard for secure electronic transactions in e-commerce developed by companies such as IBM, Microsoft, Netscope and GTE. Secure Electronic Transaction Protocol (SET) is a secure electronic delivery protocol based on the Internet (Internet), which provides a set of process specifications for electronic transactions. The SET protocol can realize encryption, authentication, and key management mechanisms in e-commerce transactions, ensuring the security of online shopping using credit cards on the Internet. 安全电子交易协议 (Secure Electronic Transaction，SET) 由威士 (VISA) 国际组织、万事达 (Master Card) 国际组织创建，结合 IBM、Microsoft、Netscope、GTE 等公司制定的电子商务中安全电子交易的一个国际标准。安全电子交易协议 SET 是一种应用于 Internet 环境下，以信用卡为基础的安全电子交付协议，它给出了一套电子交易的过程规范。通过 SET 协议可以实现电子商务交易中的加密、认证、密钥管理机制等，保证使用信用卡进行在线购物的安全。
数字签名 Digital signature	A digital signature is a mathematical scheme for demonstrating the authenticity of digital messages or documents. A valid digital signature gives a recipient reason to believe that the message was created by a known sender (authentication), that the sender cannot deny having sent the message (non-repudiation), and that the message was not altered in transit (integrity). Digital signatures are a standard element of most cryptographic protocol suites, and are commonly used for software distribution, financial transactions, contract management software, and in other cases where it is important to detect forgery or tampering. 数字签名（又称公钥数字签名、电子签章）是一种类似写在纸上的普通物理签名，但是使用了公钥加密领域的技术实现，用于鉴别数字信息的方法。一套数字签名通常定义两种互补的运算，一个用于签名，另一个用于验证。数字签名，就是只有信息的发送者才能产生的别人无法伪造的一段数字串，这段数字串同时也是对信息的发送者发送信息真实性的一个有效证明。数字签名是大多数加密协议套件的标准元素，通常用于软件分发、金融交易、合同管理软件，以及其他重要的检测伪造或篡改的情况。
数字证书 Public key certificate	In cryptography, a public key certificate, also known as a digital certificate or identity certificate, is an electronic document used to prove the ownership of a public key. The certificate includes information about the key, information about the identity of its owner (called the subject), and the digital signature of an entity that has verified the certificate's contents (called the issuer). If the signature is valid, and the software examining the certificate trusts the issuer, then it can use that key to communicate securely with the certificate's subject. 数字证书就是互联网通信中标志通信各方身份信息的一串数字，提供了一种在 Internet 上验证通信实体身份的方式，数字证书不是数字身份证，而是身份认证机构盖在数字身份证上的一个章或印（或者说加在数字身份证上的一个签名）。它是由权威机构——CA 机构，又称为证书授权（Certificate Authority）中心发行的，人们可以在网上用它来识别对方的身份。

续表

国际贸易 International Trade	International trade is the exchange of capital, goods, and services across international borders or territories. In most countries, such trade represents a significant share of gross domestic product (GDP). While international trade has existed throughout history (for example Uttarapatha, Silk Road, Amber Road, scramble for Africa, Atlantic slave trade, salt roads), its economic, social, and political importance has been on the rise in recent centuries. 国际贸易也称通商，是指跨越国境的货品和服务交易，一般由进口贸易和出口贸易组成，因此也可称之为进出口贸易。进出口贸易可以调节国内生产要素的利用率，改善国际间的供求关系，调整经济结构，增加财政收入等。
过境贸易 Transit trade	Transit trade is the transit of goods from producer to consumer, passing through other countries, for transit trade. Where the goods are not stored in the customs warehouse, they are directly transported out of the country, known as direct transit trade. If the customs warehouse is stored and transported to another country, it is called indirect transit trade. 过境贸易是商品由生产国运往消费国途经其他国家，对途经国家来说，即为过境贸易。商品入境后不存放海关仓库就直接运出国境的，称为直接过境贸易；若存放海关仓库后未经加工整理又运往另一国的，称为间接过境贸易。
业务外包 Outsourcing	Business outsourcing is also called resource outsourcing and resource externalization. It refers to the Management mode where enterprise's integration of its best external professional resources to achieve cost reduction, efficiency improvement, full play of its core competitiveness and enhance the company's ability to respond quickly to the environment. In order to obtain more competitive advantages than simply using internal resources, enterprises will submit their non-core business to the cooperative enterprise. 业务外包也称资源外包、资源外置，它是指企业整合运用其外部最优秀的专业化资源，从而达到降低成本、提高效率、充分发挥自身核心竞争力和增强企业对环境的迅速应变能力的一种管理模式。企业为了获得比单纯利用内部资源更多的竞争优势，将其非核心业务交由合作企业完成。
自由贸易 Free trade	Free trade refers to the removal of restrictions and obstacles on the import and export trade by the state, the abolition of various privileges and concessions on import and export commodities of the country, the free import and export of goods, and the free competition in domestic and foreign markets. 自由贸易，就是指国家取消对进出口贸易的限制和障碍，取消对本国进出口商品的各种特权和优惠，使商品自由地进出口，在国内外市场上自由竞争。
进口配额 Import quotas system	An import quota is a type of trade restriction that sets a physical limit on the quantity of a good that can be imported into a country in a given period of time. Quotas, like other trade restrictions, are typically used to benefit the producers of a good in that economy. 进口配额又称进口限额。它是一国政府在一定时间内，对于某些商品一定时期内的进口数量或金额，事先加以规定的限额。超过规定限额的不准进口。

续表

贸易顺差 trade surplus	If a country exports a greater value than it imports, it has a trade surplus, positive balance, or a "favourable balance". 贸易顺差是指在特定年度一国出口贸易总额大于进口贸易总额，又称"出超"。
贸易逆差 Trade deficit	if a country imports a greater value than it exports, it has a trade deficit, negative balance, "unfavorable balance", or, informally, a "trade gap". 贸易逆差亦称"贸易入超"，是国家或地区在一定时期内的进口额大于出口额的现象。一般表明一国的对外贸易处于较为不利的地位。
技术性贸易壁垒 Technical barriers to trade	Technical barriers to trade (TBTs), a category of nontariff barriers to trade, are the widely divergent measures that countries use to regulate markets, protect their consumers, or preserve their natural resources (among other objectives), but they also can be used (or perceived by foreign countries) to discriminate against imports in order to protect domestic industries. 技术性贸易壁垒，又称技术性贸易措施或技术壁垒（技术性贸易壁垒与技术壁垒不同，技术壁垒仅仅是指科学技术上的关卡，而技术性贸易壁垒则包括了技术壁垒和以技术为名的贸易壁垒），是以国家或地区的技术法规、协议、标准和认证体系（合格评定程序）等形式出现，涉及的内容广泛，涵盖科学技术、卫生、检疫、安全、环保、产品质量和认证等诸多技术性指标体系，运用于国际贸易当中，呈现出灵活多变、名目繁多的规定。
贸易保护主义 Trade protectionism	Trade protectionism is a theory of international trade. It refers to the idea and policy of restricting imports in foreign trade to protect domestic goods from foreign goods in the domestic market and providing various preferential products to domestic goods to enhance their international competitiveness. . In terms of restricting imports, trade protectionism mainly adopts two measures: tariff barriers and non-tariff barriers. The former mainly prevents large-scale imports of foreign goods by imposing high import tariffs; the latter includes a series of non-tariff measures such as import licensing system and import quota system to restrict the free import of foreign goods. 贸易保护主义是一种国际贸易理论，是指在对外贸易中实行限制进口以保护本国商品在国内市场免受外国商品竞争，并向本国商品提供各种优惠以增强其国际竞争力的主张和政策。贸易保护主义在限制进口方面，主要是采取关税壁垒和非关税壁垒两种措施。前者主要是通过征收高额进口关税阻止外国商品的大量进口；后者则包括采取进口许可证制、进口配额制等一系列非关税措施来限制外国商品自由进口。
贸易战 Trade war	Trade wars, also known as "commercial wars", refer to a series of retaliation and anti-retaliation measures where countries impose tariff barriers and non-tariff barriers to restrict the entry of goods from other countries into their domestic markets, while at the same time competing for foreign markets through dumping and foreign exchange depreciation. 贸易战又称"商战"，指的是一些国家通过高筑关税壁垒和非关税壁垒，限制别国商品进入本国市场，同时又通过倾销和外汇贬值等措施争夺国外市场，由此引起的一系列报复和反报复措施。

续表

国际物流 International logistics	International logistics, also known as global logistics, refers to an international commodity transaction or exchange activity in which materials are physically moved to overcome the space and time distance between production and consumption when production and consumption are carried out independently in two or more countries. Thus, the final purpose of the international commodity trading is completed, namely the seller deliver documents, goods and payment, and the buyer to accept the documents and make payment and collect the goods trade convection conditions. 国际物流又称全球物流，是指生产和消费分别在两个或两个以上的国家独立进行时，为克服生产和消费之间的空间距离和时间距离，对物资进行物理性移动的一项国际商品交易或交流活动，从而完成国际商品交易的最终目的，即实现卖方交付单证、货物和收取货款，而买方接收单证、支付货款和收取货物的贸易对流条件。
电子商务平台 E-commerce platform	The e-commerce platform is a platform for companies or individuals to provide online trading negotiations. The enterprise e-commerce platform is a virtual network space for business activities established on the Internet and a management environment for ensuring the smooth operation of business. It is an important place for coordinating and integrating information flow, cargo flow, orderly flow, correlation, and efficient flow of funds. Enterprises and merchants can make full use of the shared resources such as network infrastructure, payment platform, security platform and management platform provided by e-commerce platform to carry out their own business activities effectively and at low cost. 电子商务平台是一个为企业或个人提供网上交易洽谈的平台。企业电子商务平台是建立在 Internet 上进行商务活动的虚拟网络空间和保障商务顺利运营的管理环境；是协调、整合信息流、货物流、资金流有序、关联、高效流动的重要场所。企业、商家可充分利用电子商务平台提供的网络基础设施、支付平台、安全平台、管理平台等共享资源有效地、低成本地开展自己的商业活动。
跨境电子商务 Cross-border e-commerce	Cross-border e-commerce refers to an international business activity that is divided into transaction entities of different customs, through transactions through e-commerce platforms, payment settlement, and delivery of goods through cross-border logistics. 跨境电子商务是指分属不同关境的交易主体，通过电子商务平台达成交易、进行支付结算，并通过跨境物流送达商品、完成交易的一种国际商业活动。
电子商务协议 An e-commerce agreement	An e-commerce agreement is an agreement designed to fulfill e-commerce activities. A Protocol is a series of steps taken by two or more participants to accomplish a particular task. Currently, the widely used electronic commerce protocols include Secure Socket Layer, Secure electronic Transaction protocol SET(SecureElectronic Transaction), IBS protocol based on public key system, non-repudiation protocol, etc. 电子商务协议是为了完成电子商务活动而设计的协议，而所谓协议就是两个或两个以上的参与者为完成某项特定的任务而采取的一系列步骤。目前，得到广泛应用的电子商务协议有安全套接层协议 SSL(Secure Socket Layer)、安全电子交易协议 SET(SecureElectronic Transaction)、基于公钥体制的 IBS 协议、非否认协议等。

续表

旅游电子商务 Tourism electronic commerce	Tourism e-commerce refers to the business system that uses the most popular electronic means to operate the tourism industry and its distribution system based on the network and the tourism information base and electronic business bank. Tourism e-commerce provides an Internet platform for the vast number of tourism industry peers. 旅游电子商务是指以网络为主体，以旅游信息库、电子化商务银行为基础，利用最先进的电子手段运作旅游业及其分销系统的商务体系。旅游电子商务为广大旅游业同行提供了一个互联网的平台。
医药电子商务 Pharmaceutical e-commerce	Pharmaceutical e-commerce refers to the behavior of the exchange of pharmaceutical products and provide related services by profit-oriented market economy entity including medical institutions, pharmaceutical companies, banks, pharmaceutical manufacturers, medical information service providers, third-party organizations, etc., relying on modern information such as computers and network technologies (mainly the Internet). 医药电子商务是指以医疗机构、医药公司、银行、医药生产商、医药信息服务提供商、第三方机构等以赢利为目的的市场经济主体，凭借计算机和网络技术（主要是互联网）等现代信息技术，进行医药产品交换及提供相关服务的行为。
移动电子商务 M-Commerce	Mobile e-commerce (M-Commerce), which is derived from the concept of e-commerce (E-Commerce). E-commerce uses PC as the main interface, which is wired e-commerce; while mobile e-commerce, it is through mobile phones, PDAs (personal digital assistants), which can be installed in pockets for business activities. Mobile e-commerce is B2B, B2C, C2C or O2O e-commerce using wireless terminals such as mobile phones, PDAs and handheld computers. It combines the Internet, mobile communication technology, short-range communication technology and other information processing technologies to enable people to conduct various business activities at any time and any place, realizing anytime, anywhere, online and offline shopping and trading, online electronic payments and various trading activities, business activities, financial activities and related comprehensive service activities. 移动电子商务 (M-Commerce)，它由电子商务 (E-Commerce) 的概念衍生出来，电子商务以 PC 机为主要界面，是有线的电子商务；而移动电子商务，则是通过手机、PDA 这些可以装在口袋里的终端与我们谋面，无论何时、何地都可以开始。移动电子商务就是利用手机、PDA 及掌上电脑等无线终端进行的 B2B、B2C、C2C 或 O2O 的电子商务。它将因特网、移动通信技术、短距离通信技术及其它信息处理技术完美的结合，使人们可以在任何时间、任何地点进行各种商贸活动，实现随时随地、线上线下的购物与交易、在线电子支付以及各种交易活动、商务活动、金融活动和相关的综合服务活动等。

续表

电子商务师 E-commerce engineer	E-commerce division refers to people who use computer technology, network technology, and modern information technology such as professional online business platform to help merchants and customers or businesses and businesses to engage in various business activities or related work. They are high-quality compound talents that combine IT and business knowledge. 电子商务师是指利用计算机技术、网络技术，通过专业的网络商务平台等现代信息技术，帮助商家与顾客或商家与商家之间从事各类商务活动或相关工作的人员，可以说是融 IT 与商务于一身的高素质复合型人才。
推荐系统 Recommender system	The recommendation system is to use the e-commerce website to provide product information and suggestions to customers, to help users decide what products should be purchased, and to simulate sales personnel to help customers complete the purchase process. Personalized recommendation is to recommend information and products that users are interested in based on the user's interest characteristics and purchase behavior. As the scale of e-commerce continues to expand, the number and variety of products grow rapidly, and customers need to spend a lot of time to find the products they want to buy. This kind of browsing of a large amount of unrelated information and product processes will undoubtedly cause consumers who are drowning in information overload problems to continue to lose. In order to solve these problems, a personalized recommendation system came into being. The personalized recommendation system is an advanced business intelligence platform based on massive data mining to help e-commerce websites provide fully personalized decision support and information services for their customers' shopping. 推荐系统是利用电子商务网站向客户提供商品信息和建议，帮助用户决定应该购买什么产品，模拟销售人员帮助客户完成购买过程。个性化推荐是根据用户的兴趣特点和购买行为，向用户推荐用户感兴趣的信息和商品。随着电子商务规模的不断扩大，商品个数和种类快速增长，顾客需要花费大量的时间才能找到自己想买的商品。这种浏览大量无关的信息和产品过程无疑会使淹没在信息过载问题中的消费者不断流失。为了解决这些问题，个性化推荐系统应运而生。个性化推荐系统是建立在海量数据挖掘基础上的一种高级商务智能平台，以帮助电子商务网站为其顾客购物提供完全个性化的决策支持和信息服务。
个性化推荐系统 Personalized recommen-dation system	The personalized recommendation system is the product of the development of the Internet and e-commerce. It is an advanced business intelligence platform based on massive data mining, providing customers with personalized information services and decision support. In recent years, there have been many examples of very successful large-scale recommendation systems. At the same time, personalized recommendation systems have gradually become one of the research hotspots in academia. 个性化推荐系统是互联网和电子商务发展的产物，它是建立在海量数据挖掘基础上的一种高级商务智能平台，向顾客提供个性化的信息服务和决策支持。近年来已经出现了许多非常成功的大型推荐系统实例，与此同时，个性化推荐系统也逐渐成为学术界的研究热点之一。

续表

协同过滤 Collaborative filtering	Collaborative filtering is simply a matter of recommending information of interest to a user using the preferences of a group of people who share interests and have common experience. Individuals respond to the information to a considerable extent (such as scoring) through a cooperative mechanism and record it to achieve the purpose of filtering to help others filter information. The response is not necessarily limited to particular interest, and the record of particularly uninteresting information is also very important. Collaborative filtering can be further divided into rating or social filtering. Collaborative filtering is hot in the global Internet world with its speed and robustness. 协同过滤简单来说是利用某个兴趣相投、拥有共同经验之群体的喜好来推荐用户感兴趣的信息，个人通过合作的机制给予信息相当程度的回应（如评分）并记录下来以达到过滤的目的进而帮助别人筛选信息，回应不一定局限于特别感兴趣的，特别不感兴趣信息的记录也相当重要。协同过滤又可分为评比（rating）或者群体过滤（social filtering）协同过滤以其出色的速度和健壮性，在全球互联网领域炙手可热。
移动支付 Mobile payment	Mobile payment, also known as mobile payment, is a service that allows users to use their mobile terminals (usually mobile phones) to pay for goods or services they consume. The unit or individual sends the payment instruction directly or indirectly to the banking financial institution through the mobile device, the Internet or proximity sensing to generate the money payment and the fund transfer behavior, thereby realizing the mobile payment function. Mobile payment combines terminal equipment, the Internet, application providers, and financial institutions to provide users with financial services such as money payment and payment. 移动支付也称为手机支付，就是允许用户使用其移动终端（通常是手机）对所消费的商品或服务进行账务支付的一种服务方式。单位或个人通过移动设备、互联网或者近距离传感直接或间接向银行金融机构发送支付指令产生货币支付与资金转移行为，从而实现移动支付功能。移动支付将终端设备、互联网、应用提供商以及金融机构相融合，为用户提供货币支付、缴费等金融业务。
公开密钥体系 Wireless Public Key Infrastructure(WPKI)	PKI is a public key system. Simply, PKI technology is an infrastructure that provides information security services using public key theory and technology. It is an internationally recognized security authentication mechanism for Internet e-commerce. It uses public key cryptography in modern cryptography to provide a unified technical framework for data encryption and digital signature services in an open Internet environment. PKI 即公开密钥体系，简单地说，PKI 技术就是利用公钥理论和技术建立的提供信息安全服务的基础设施，它是国际公认的互联网电子商务的安全认证机制，它利用现代密码学中的公钥密码技术在开放的 Internet 网络环境中提供数据加密以及数字签名服务的统一的技术框架。

续表

全程电子商务 Whole-process e-commerce	Whole-process e-commerce is an extension of the concept of e-commerce. The Whole-process e-commerce, whose core is the necessary management model in the electronic commerce times, through the network technology and the SaaS delivery model, provides enterprises with management, and online e-commerce services, to realize the enterprise internal management and effective collaborative business process between enterprises. It is the interaction between the enterprise and the enterprise agreement. "全程电子商务"是一个由电子商务延伸出来的概念。全程电子商务是以电子商务时代所需的管理模式为核心，通过网络技术和 SaaS 交付模式，为企业提供在线管理以及电子商务服务，实现企业内部管理以及企业之间的商务流程的有效协同，是企业与企业之间的交互协议。
亚马逊物流 Fulfillment by Amazon	FBA Logistics is a professional logistics company that provides FBA head-to-head transportation, FBA customs clearance, FBA return, short-term storage and other FBA services. It provides a one-stop service for storage, sorting, packaging, assembly, delivery and return. FBA 物流是一家专业从事及代理亚马逊 FBA 头程运输、FBA 代清关、FBA 退换标，短期仓储等 FBA 一条龙服务，提供存储，分拣，包装，装配，派送，退货一站式服务的物流模式。
亚马逊会员 Amazon Prime	Amazon Prime is a paid subscription service offered by Amazon that gives users access to free two-day delivery (one-day in some areas), streaming video and music, and other benefits for a monthly or yearly fee. 亚马逊 Prime 是亚马逊提供的付费订阅服务，用户可以享受免费的两天送货服务 (在某些地区一天)、流媒体视频和音乐，以及其他服务。它需要支付一定的月费或年费。
Gmarket	Gmarket is South Korea' s largest integrated shopping site. The total sales of goods online retail market in South Korea ranked first. It mainly sells books, MP3, cosmetics, computers, home appliances, clothing, etc. Gmarket 是韩国最大的综合购物网站，在韩国在线零售市场中的商品销售总值方面排名第一，主要销售书籍、MP3、化妆品、计算机、家电、衣服等。
汇率 Exchange rate	The exchange rate refers to the ratio or parity of a country' s currency to another country' s currency, or the price of another country' s currency expressed in one country' s currency. Changes in exchange rates have a direct regulatory effect on a country' s import and export trade. Under certain conditions, by depreciating the domestic currency against the outside world, that is, letting the exchange rate fall, it will play a role in promoting exports and restricting imports. Conversely, the appreciation of the domestic currency, that is, the rise in the exchange rate, will play a role in restricting exports and increasing imports. 汇率是指一国货币与另一国货币的比率或比价，或者说是用一国货币表示的另一国货币的价格。汇率变动对一国进出口贸易有着直接的调节作用。在一定条件下，通过使本国货币对外贬值，即让汇率下降，会起到促进出口、限制进口的作用；反之，本国货币对外升值，即汇率上升，则起到限制出口、增加进口的作用。

续表

大数据营销 Account-based marketing	Account-based marketing (ABM), also known as key account marketing, is a strategic approach to business marketing based on account awareness in which an organization considers and communicates with individual prospect or customer accounts as markets of one. Account-based marketing is typically employed in enterprise level sales organizations. 基于数据的市场营销 (ABM)，也被称为“大数据营销”，是一种基于数据意识的企业营销战略方法，该组织考虑并与单个客户或客户账户进行沟通，作为一个市场。基于数据的营销通常在企业级的销售组织中使用。
信用卡 Credit Card	A credit card, also called a credit card, is a non-cash transaction payment method and is a simple credit service. The credit card is issued by the bank or credit card company according to the user’s credit and financial resources. The cardholder does not need to pay cash when using the credit card, and then repay the bill on the day of the bill. 信用卡，又叫贷记卡。是一种非现金交易付款的方式，是简单的信贷服务。信用卡由银行或信用卡公司依照用户的信用度与财力发给持卡人，持卡人持信用卡消费时无须支付现金，待账单日时再进行还款。
秒杀 Second kill	“Second kill” means the online sellers sell some ultra-low price goods and all buyers online buy at the same time. Popularly speaking, it is the online time-limit panic buying activities for promotion purposes. Because goods are cheap, they are often snapped up as soon as they hit the shelves, sometimes in a second. “秒杀”，就是网络卖家发布一些超低价格的商品，所有买家在同一时间网上抢购的一种销售方式。通俗一点讲就是网络商家为促销等目的组织的网上限时抢购活动。由于商品价格低廉，往往一上架就被抢购一空，有时只用一秒钟。
购买力 Purchasing power	Purchasing power is an important factor that constitutes the market and affects the size of the market, while purchasing power is constrained by the macroeconomic environment and is a reflection of the economic environment. The main factors influencing purchasing power include real income, currency value, consumer savings and credit, consumer spending patterns and so on. 购买力是构成市场和影响市场规模大小的重要因素，而购买力是受宏观经济环境制约的，是经济环境的反映。影响购买力的主要因素有居民的实际收入、币值、消费者的储蓄和信用、消费者的支出模式等。
客户关系管理 Customer relationship management	CRM is customer relationship management, which means that enterprises use CRM technology to manage the relationship with customers. In different situations, CRM may be a management term, which may be a software system. Generally referred to as CRM, a software system that automates the analysis of sales, marketing, customer service, and applications processes using a computer. Its goal is to reduce sales cycle and cost of sales, increase revenue, and find new markets and channels needed to expand your business by increasing customer value, satisfaction, profitability and loyalty. CRM is a business strategy for selecting and managing valued customers and their relationships. CRM requires a customer-centric culture to support effective marketing, sales and service processes.

续表

客户关系管理 Customer relationship management	CRM 即客户关系管理，是指企业用 CRM 技术来管理与客户之间的关系。在不同场合下，CRM 可能是一个管理学术语，也可能是一个软件系统。通常所指的 CRM，指用计算机自动化分析销售、市场营销、客户服务以及应用等流程的软件系统。它的目标是通过提高客户的价值、满意度、营利性和忠实度来缩减销售周期和销售成本、增加收入、寻找扩展业务所需的新的市场和渠道。CRM 是选择和管理有价值客户及其关系的一种商业策略，CRM 要求以客户为中心的企业文化来支持有效的市场营销、销售与服务流程。
购物车 Shopping Cart	The buyer can add and delete the goods as it is in the supermarket, and then place the order after purchase. Shopping cart should be able to track the goods selected by customers, record the selected products, and can update them at any time, which can be paid for and can provide great convenience to customers. 网上商店所说的购物车是与现实的购物车相比，买家可以像在超市里购物一样，随意添加、删除商品，选购完毕后，统一下单。购物车能跟踪顾客所选的商品，记录所选商品，还能随时更新，能给顾客提供很大的方便。
线上营销 Online Marketing	Online marketing is to entrust the network marketing work that originally needed the company’s own employees to the professional network marketing service provider by contract. Using the Internet as a platform and based on the analysis of the current situation, product characteristics and industry characteristics, the network marketing outsourcing service provider has tailor-made personalized and cost-effective network marketing solutions. It is fully responsible for the effective implementation of the program, tracking and monitoring the effectiveness of network marketing, and regularly providing performance analysis reports for enterprises. In this process, the network marketing service provider will give full play to its various professional advantages in technology, marketing planning, implementation, etc., and do everything in its power to complete the predetermined goals to obtain the service fees paid by the enterprise. 线上营销就是把原本需要企业自己雇人实现的网络营销工作以合同的方式委托给专业网络营销服务商。网络营销外包服务商以互联网为平台，在深入分析企业现状、产品特点和行业特征的基础上，为企业量身定制个性化的高性价比网络营销方案，全面负责方案的有效实施，对网络营销效果进行跟踪监控，并定期为企业提供效果分析报告。在这个过程中网络营销服务商会充分发挥其在技术、营销策划、实施等方面上的各种专业优势，竭尽所能完成预定的目标以获得企业支付的服务费用。
社会化媒体营销 Social media marketing	Social media marketing, also known as social marketing, is a way to use marketing, online communities, blogs, encyclopedias or other Internet collaboration platforms to conduct marketing, public relations and customer service development. It is also known as social media marketing, social media marketing, social media integrated marketing, and popular weak relationship marketing. In online marketing, social media mainly refers to a comprehensive site with network nature, and their content is provided by users voluntarily, rather than direct employment relationship.

续表

社会化媒体营销 Social media marketing	社会化媒体营销又称社会化营销，是利用社会化网络，如在线社区，博客，百科或者其他互联网协作平台媒体来进行营销，是公共关系和客户服务维护开拓的一种方式。在网络营销中，社会化媒体主要是指一个具有网络性质的综合站点，而它们的内容都是由用户自愿提供的，而不是直接的雇佣关系。
横幅广告 Web banner	A web banner or banner ad is a form of advertising on the World Wide Web delivered by an ad server. In many cases, banners are delivered by a central ad server. When the advertiser scans their logfiles and detects that a web user has visited the advertiser's site from the content site by clicking on the banner ad, the advertiser sends the content provider some small amount of money (usually around five to ten US cents). 横幅广告是网络广告最早采用的形式，也是目前最常见的形式。横幅广告又称旗帜广告，它是横跨于网页上的矩形公告牌，当用户点击这些横幅的时候，通常可以链接到广告主的网页，而广告主会给内容商一定数额的佣金（通常为 5 ～ 10 美分）。
网站流量 Web traffic	Web traffic is the amount of data sent and received by visitors to a website. This necessarily does not include the traffic generated by bots. This is determined by the number of visitors and the number of pages they visit. Sites monitor the incoming and outgoing traffic to see which parts or pages of their site are popular and if there are any apparent trends, such as one specific page being viewed mostly by people in a particular country. 网站流量是访问者发送和接收到的数据量。这必然不包括由自动程序产生的流量。这是由访问者的数量和他们访问的页面数量决定的。站点可以监控传入和传出的流量，以查看其站点的哪些部分或页面是受欢迎的，如果有任何明显的趋势，比如某个特定国家的人主要查看某个特定页面。
推荐营销 Referral marketing	Referral marketing is a method of promoting products or services to new customers through referrals, usually word of mouth. Such referrals often happen spontaneously but businesses can influence this through appropriate strategies. 推荐营销是一种通过推荐的方式向新客户推销产品或服务的方法，通常是口碑营销。这种推荐通常是自发进行的，而且企业可以通过适当的策略来影响这种情况。
原生广告 Native advertising	Native advertising is a type of advertising, mostly online, that matches the form and function of the platform upon which it appears. In many cases, it manifests as either an article or video, produced by an advertiser with the specific intent to promote a product, while matching the form and style which would otherwise be seen in the work of the platform's editorial staff. The word "native" refers to this coherence of the content with the other media that appears on the platform. 原生广告是一种广告，主要是在线广告，它与它出现的平台的形式和功能相匹配。在许多情况下，它表现为一篇文章或一段视频，由一个广告主制作，目的是推销一种产品，同时与该平台的编辑人员在工作中看到的形式和风格相匹配。

续表

内容营销 Content marketing	Content marketing is a form of marketing focused on creating, publishing, and distributing content for a targeted audience online. Content marketing refers to the use of pictures, text, animations, etc. to convey relevant content of the company to the customer information and promote sales. It realizes the purpose of network marketing by transmitting valuable information to users through reasonable content creation, distribution and dissemination. The carrier they are attached to can be the company's LOGO (VI), albums, websites, advertisements, and even T-shirts, paper cups, handbags, etc. According to different carriers, the mediums are different, but the core of the content must be consistent. It is often used by businesses in order to attract attention and generate leads, expand their customer base, generate or increase online sales, increase brand awareness or credibility and engage an online community of users. 内容营销，指的是以图片、文字、动画等介质传达有关企业的相关内容给客户，通过合理的内容创建、发布及传播，向用户传递有价值的信息，从而实现网络营销的目的。他们所依附的载体，可以是企业的LOGO（VI）、画册、网站、广告，甚至是T恤、纸杯、手提袋等，根据不同的载体，传递的介质各有不同，但是内容的核心必须是一致的。它经常被企业用于：吸引注意力，扩大他们的客户基础，产生或增加在线销售，提高品牌知名度或可信度，并吸引一个在线社区的用户。
独立访问者 Unique visitors	A unique visitor refers to the number of different individuals requesting a page from a website for a given period of time, regardless of the frequency of their visits. Access refers to the number of visits to the site, no matter how many times visitors visit. 独立访问者指的是在给定的时间段内，从网站请求页面的不同个体的数量，无论他们访问的频率如何。访问指的是访问站点的次数，无论访问者访问多少次。
千人成本 Cost Per Mille	Cost per mille (CPM) refers to the average cost of advertising for each person who hears or sees an ad during the ad serving process. Traditional media often use this pricing method. It is used in marketing as a benchmark metric to calculate the relative cost of advertising campaigns or advertising information in a given medium. CPM(千人成本)指的是广告投放过程中，听到或者看到某广告的每一人平均分担到多少广告成本。传统媒介多采用这种计价方式。它在市场营销中作为基准度量来计算广告活动或广告信息在给定媒介中的相对成本。
电子化采购 E-procurement	E-procurement is an inter-enterprise purchase using the Internet, electronic data interchange, or electronic file transfer. Suppliers and buyers send queries, orders, invoices, payments, etc. directly through their computer systems. 电子化采购是使用因特网、电子数据互换或电子文件传输来进行的企业间采购行为。供方和买方直接通过计算机系统，传送查询信息、订单、发票、支付信息等。

续表

关键词竞价广告 AdWords	Google AdWords is an online advertising service developed by Google, where advertisers pay to display brief advertising copy, product listings, and video content within the Google ad network to web users. Google AdWords' system is based partly on cookies and partly on keywords determined by advertisers. Google uses these characteristics to place advertising copy on pages where they think it might be relevant. Advertisers pay when users divert their browsing to click on the advertising copy. Partner websites receive a portion of the generated income. 搜索引擎 Google 的关键词竞价广告称为 AdWords，也称为"赞助商链接"，中文俗称"Google 右侧广告"。AdWords 是一种快速简单的购买广告服务的方式，这种广告服务的针对性强，无论您的预算是多少，它都按每次点击计费 (CPC)。谷歌 AdWords 的系统部分基于 cookie，部分基于广告商决定的关键词。谷歌利用这些特性将广告放在他们认为相关的页面上。
跳出率 Bounce rate	Bounce rate (sometimes confused with exit rate) is an Internet marketing term used in web traffic analysis. It represents the percentage of visitors who enter the site and then leave ("bounce") rather than continuing to view other pages within the same site. Bounce rate is a measure of the effectiveness of a website in encouraging visitors to continue with their visit. It is expressed as a percentage and represents the proportion of visits that end on the first page of the website that the visitor sees. 跳出率指用户通过搜索关键词跳转到网站，仅浏览了一个页面就离开的访问次数与所有访问次数的百分比。观察关键词的跳出率就可以得知用户对网站内容的认可，或者说网站是否对用户有吸引力。而网站的内容是否能够对用户有所帮助留住用户也直接可以直接在跳出率中看出来，所以跳出率是衡量网站内容质量的重要标准。
投资回报率 Return on investment	Return on investment (ROI) is the value that should be returned through investment, that is, the economic return that a company receives from an investment activity. It covers the profitability goals of the company. Profits are related to the property necessary to operate, because managers must make a profit through investment and existing property. 投资回报率（ROI）是指通过投资而应返回的价值，即企业从一项投资活动中得到的经济回报。它涵盖了企业的获利目标。利润和投入经营所必备的财产相关，因为管理人员必须通过投资和现有财产获得利润。
校园电子商务 Campus e-commerce	Campus e-commerce is a process in which teachers and students use the Internet to provide and purchase products, services and information. Specific speaking, the campus e-commerce is electronic commerce on the concrete application of the special environment. It refers to the campus within the scope of use of basic network, computer hardware, software and electronic communications to build units of content with the campus, the enterprise or individual business, work, study and life activity. 校园电子商务就是在校师生利用网络来提供和购买产品、服务和信息的过程。具体来讲，校园电子商务是电子商务在校园这个特殊环境下的具体应用，它是指在校园范围内利用基础网络、计算机硬件、软件和电子通信手段构建的满足于校园内单位、企业或个人进行商务、工作、学习、生活各方面活动需要的一个高可用性、伸缩性和安全性的计算机系统。

续表

虚假交易 Fake trading	Fake trading, as the name implies, refers to the non-existence, unreal trading behavior. On the Internet, it generally refers to use improper ways for commodity sales, to rise store rating or credit score, which does harm to consumers' rights. It is Also called "credit speculation" "brush diamond" "brush credibility" "brush credit" . 虚假交易，顾名思义，指不存在、不真实的买卖行为。在互联网中，一般指在淘宝、拍拍等网络购物平台中通过不正当方式获得商品销量、店铺评分、信用积分等不当利益，妨害买家权益行为。又称“信用炒作”“刷钻”“刷信誉”“刷信用”。
供应商 Supplier	Suppliers are enterprises and individuals that supply enterprises and their competitors with all kinds of resources needed, including raw materials, equipment, energy, labor services and capital. How they can have a significant impact on enterprise' s marketing activity, such as shortage of raw material price change, will affect the enterprise product price and delivery time, and thus weaken the enterprise long-term cooperation with customers and interests, 供应商是向企业及其竞争对手供应各种所需资源的企业和个人，包括提供原材料、设备、能源、劳务和资金等。它们的情况会对企业的营销活动产生巨大的影响，如原材料价格变化、短缺等都会影响企业产品的价格和交货期，并会因此削弱企业与客户的长期合作与利益。
B2G Business-to-government	The B2G model is an e-commerce between the enterprise and the government management department, such as government procurement, customs tax filing platform, and the tax bureau of the State Administration of Taxation and the local tax bureau. B2G 模式是企业与政府管理部门之间的电子商务，如政府采购、海关报税的平台，国税局和地税局报税的平台等。
页面浏览量 Page view	PV (page view) is the number of page views, usually the main indicator for measuring a network news channel or website or even a network news. The number of page views is one of the most commonly used indicators for evaluating website traffic, referred to as PV. PV（page view）即页面浏览量，通常是衡量一个网络新闻频道或网站甚至一条网络新闻的主要指标。网页浏览数是评价网站流量最常用的指标之一，简称为 PV。
转化率 Conversion Rate	Conversion rate is the percentage of visitors who visit a site and convert visitors to all visitors. 转化率指访问某一网站访客中，转化的访客占全部访客的比例。
按行为付费 Cost Per Action	Cost per acquisition (CPA), also known as "Cost per action" or pay per acquisition (PPA) and cost per conversion, is an online advertising pricing model where the advertiser pays for a specified acquisition - for example a sale, click, or form submit (e.g., contact request, newsletter sign up, registration etc.) CPA（Cost Per Action）是一种广告计费模式，顾名思义按照行为作为指标来计费，这个行为可以是注册、咨询、放入购物车等。广告公司和媒体公司常用 CPA、CPC、CPM 一起来衡量广告价格。

References

[1] Dr. Henrik B. Okholm, Partner Martin H. Thelle, Partner Anna Möller, Senior Economist Dr. Bruno Basalisco, Economist Signe Rølmer, Economist. E-commerce and delivery--A study of the state of play of EU parcel markets with particular emphasis on e-commerce[DB/OL]. https://www.copenhageneconomics.com/dyn/resources/Publication/publicationPDF/8/238/0/E-commerce-and-delivery.pdf, 2013.

[2] The European Consumer Centres' Network. Online Cross-Border Mystery Shopping-State Of The E-Union[DB/OL]. https://ec.europa.eu/info/sites/info/files/mystery_shopping_report_2011_en.pdf,2011.

[3] Hang Y. Analysis on the Electronic Commerce Talent Training Mode for Application Oriented University under the Environment of Masses Entrepreneurship and Innovation[J]. DEStech Transactions on Social Science, Education and Human Science, 2016.

[4] Huang W, Zhou S. Electronic Commerce Innovation and Development Strategy of Travel Agency Under Low-Carbon Economy[M]// Proceedings of the International Conference on Information Engineering and Applications (IEA) 2012. Springer London, 2013:399-406.

[5] 陶莉莉 . 基于电子商务环境下的物流管理模式 [J]. 商场现代化 ,2013(27):93.

[6] 孙艳艳 . 我国跨境电子商务的发展现状分析 [J]. 现代经济信息 ,2014(15):169-170.

[7] 高博咨询 . 杭州跨境贸易电子商务产业发展规划报告 [R]. 杭州 : 杭州高博技术与战略研究所 ,2014.

[8] 张夏恒 , 马天山 . 中国跨境电子商务物流困境及对策建议 [J]. 当代经济管理，2015(5):41-45.

[9] 孟祥铭 , 汤倩慧 . 中国跨境贸易电子商务发展现状与对策分析 [J]. 沈阳工业大学学报：社会科学版，2014，7(02):120-125.

[10] 鄂立彬，黄永稳 . 国际贸易新方式 : 跨境电子商务的最新研究 [J]. 东北财经大学学报，2014(2):22-31.

[11] 叶华 . 浅谈中国外贸跨境电子商务的发展 [J]. 湖北经济学院学报：人文社会科学版，2013 (11):50-51.

[12] 张灿 . 重庆跨境电商发展现状分析及对策建议 [J]. 重庆科技学院学报：社会科学版，2016(05):57-59.

[13] 朱启松 , 朱慧婷 . "互联网 +" 背景下跨境电商发展的 SWOT 分析：以重庆为例 [J]. 四川理工学院学报：社会科学版，2016，31(05):73-82.

[14] 李金芳，陈夏林，吴来恩，等 . M2B2C 跨境电商出口模式的产业功能及实现：以中国 (杭州) 跨境电子商务综合试验区为例 [J]. 中共杭州市委党校学报，2015(05):90-96.

[15] 徐艳，严怀旭．跨境电子商务模式研究 [J]. 中国市场，2015(16):144-146.
[16] 涂萍萍．电子商务税收法律问题研究 [D]. 厦门：厦门大学，2014.
[17] 樊晓云．我国跨境外贸电商平台模式比较分析与选择 [J]. 对外经贸，2015(02):12-14.
[18] 偰娜．我国跨境电子商务贸易平台模式探讨 [J]. 中国流通经济，2015(08):70-74.
[19] 朱林婷．第三方跨境支付的问题及发展对策研究 [J]. 特区经济，2014(06):103-104.
[20] 石惠文．第三方支付平台跨境支付业务监管问题研究 [J]. 全国商情：经济理论研究，2015(16):29-30.
[21] 吴崇攀，王佳．第三方支付跨境业务洗钱风险分析及对策 [J]. 海南金融，2015(10):53-55.
[22] 李海莲，陈荣红．跨境电子商务通关制度的国际比较及其完善路径研究 [J]. 国际商务：对外经济贸易大学学报，2015(03):112-120.
[23] 鄂立彬，刘智勇．跨境电子商务阳光化通关问题研究 [J]. 国际贸易，2014(09):32-34.
[24] 李迟．跨境电商问题、对策与发展趋势研究 [J]. 浙江工商职业技术学院学报，2015(02):25-28.
[25] 武玥，王铸东，杨晓璇．跨境电子商务发展趋势及对我国外贸转型升级的促进作用 [J]. 商业经济研究，2015(23):63-65.
[26] 康莹．跨境电商现状分析及趋势探讨 [J]. 现代经济信息，2015(14):335.
[27] 张红英．中国 B2C 跨境电子商务的发展问题研究 [D]. 济南：山东大学，2014.
[28] 杨璐．电子商务对我国对外贸易的影响及对策研究 [D]. 合肥：安徽大学，2014.
[29] 常成．跨境电子商务与贸易增长的互动关系研究 [D]. 沈阳：沈阳工业大学，2015.
[30] 穆承刚．我国小额跨境电子商务模式研究 [D]. 上海：上海社会科学院，2014.
[31] 孙蕾，王芳．中国跨境电子商务发展现状及对策 [J]. 中国流通经济，2015(03):38-41.
[32] 刘圆．跨境电子商务背景下我国海关税收征管模式优化的研究 [D]. 上海：上海海关学院，2015.
[33] 王睦欣．全球电子商务发展新态势与中国电子商务创新发展 [D]. 长春：吉林大学，2015.
[34] 李兵．论电子商务的特点与影响 [J]. 山东经济，2001(01):78-80.
[35] 赫永军．我国跨境电商的发展现状及问题研究 [D]. 长春：东北师范大学，2017.